TOEFL Vocabulary Builder:

Ace the TOEFL with 500+ Essential Vocab Words

Jackie Bolen

www.eslspeaking.org

Table of Contents

About the Author: Jackie Bolen...6

How to Use this Book 7

Top 10 Tips to Prepare for the TOEFL Exam.......................................8

Brash and Aggressive...12

Sam's Dissertation..14

Add insult to injury..16

A dime a dozen...16

A piece of cake...16

A tough pill to swallow (A bitter pill to swallow)................................17

Beat around the bush..17

Widespread Abuse..18

Ample Time...20

Beef Up..22

Vanished Into Thin Air...24

Hard to Decipher...26

In the Ballpark 28

Chronological Order 30

Rigid Thinking...32

Confusing Words: Accept/Except 34

What's the Verdict?...36

A Dilemma..38

Lab Homework 40

Advocate for Yourself 42

Noise Pollution..44

Shades of Gray 46

Behind the scenes..48

Better late than never..48

Break the bank...48

Burning the midnight oil...49

Burn the candle at both ends...49

Dry Up..50

Confusing Words: Adverse/Averse...52

Scrutinize Carefully...54

Writing Homework...56

A Few Qualms 58

Applying for University 60

Cumbersome..62

Break Through..64

Ph.D Options..66

Bury my head in the sand..68

Call it a day...68

Calm before the storm...68

Can't put my finger on it...69

Compare apples to oranges...69

Famine 70

Protecting the Environment..72

Survey Design..74

An Ethical Issue..76

Fundamental Flaws..78
Lifestyle Changes...80
Confusing Words: Bored/Boring..82
Hold On...84
The Environment..86
At Risk...88
Corner the market...90
Crunch the numbers..90
Fall through the cracks...90
Feeling the pinch...91
Get into deep water...91
Key Role..92
For the Long Haul...94
Confusing Words: e.g. / i.e...96
Indefatigable...98
Knowledge-Based Economy..100
In the Black..102
Evolution...104
Housing in Vancouver..106
Pull It Off..108
Confusing Words: For/Since..110
Private Industry...112
Give them a run for their money..114
Go the extra mile..114
Hit the books...114
In the driver's seat..115
In the same boat..115
Graduate from College..116
Experts...118
Tariffs..120
Confusing Words: Imply/Infer...122
Cover Up...124
Climate Change...126
The Start-Up..128
Give Out..130
It's not rocket science...132
It's time to face the music...132
It takes two to tango..132
Keep this under wraps...133
Keep your head above water...133
Confusing Words: Sight/Site/Cite...134
Talking About Strategy...136
Cheating...138
By No Means...140
Balance of Power..142
Gold Standard...144
Factory Farms..146
Erroneous Assumptions..148
Confusing Words: Who/Which/That..150
At a Standstill..152

Land on your feet..154
Learn the ropes...154
Let off the hook..154
Making a mountain out of a molehill..155
Make ends meet..155
Swallow My Pride...156
Before You Go...158

About the Author: Jackie Bolen

I taught English in South Korea for 10 years to every level and type of student. I've taught every age from kindergarten kids to adults. These days, I'm teaching in Vancouver, Canada.

I hold a Master of Arts in Psychology. During my time in Korea I successfully completed the CELTA and DELTA teaching certification programs. With the combination of 20 years teaching ESL/EFL learners of all ages and levels, and the more formal teaching qualifications I've obtained, I have a solid foundation on which to offer advice to English learners.

I hope that you find this book useful. Please send me an email with any questions or feedback that you might have. And please don't forget to join my email list for useful tips for learning English: www.eslspeaking.org/learn-english.

YouTube: www.youtube.com/c/jackiebolen

Pinterest: www.pinterest.com/eslspeaking

Email: jb.business.online@gmail.com

You may also want to check out these other resources (also by Jackie Bolen). It's easy to find them wherever you like to buy books.

- 365 American English Idioms

- Advanced English Conversation Dialogues

- English Vocabulary Masterclass for TOEFL, TOEIC, IELTS, and CELPIP

How to Use this Book

This book is designed to help you build a bigger vocabulary, especially academic English, which is essential for the TOEFL exam. If you want to get a high score on this exam, it will be necessary to know this kind of language.

To use this book, I recommend doing one lesson per day, instead of all of them at one time. This will help you to remember the material. There are about 10 weeks of lessons. Do the practice exercises, and try not to cheat by looking at the answers!

Use a vocabulary notebook, and be sure to write down any new words that you learn. Review them frequently and consider making some flashcards. Push yourself to use this new vocabulary when speaking and see if you can find them when watching English TV or movies, or reading.

Make sure you know how to pronounce any new word that you learn. Look on YouTube or Google, "How to say _____" to find out. This will help you get a higher score on the speaking section.

This book is one way to expand your vocabulary range. You might also consider extensive reading and listening as well. Find things to listen to (podcasts, movies, TV shows) or read (books, magazine, newspaper articles) that are at your level, or just slightly below. The key is to read or listen just for fun and to not have to use a dictionary all the time. This will not only help you become more familiar with English vocabulary but it'll also help you improve your grammatical accuracy as well.

Be sure to do some practice tests (search on Google for "TOEFL practice test") and record yourself for the speaking section to review later. Try to use the new vocabulary that you've acquired in this book.

Top 10 Tips to Prepare for the TOEFL Exam

If you want to get a high score on the TOEFL exam, here are some tips to pay attention to.

#1: Learn the Test Format

Knowing what to expect on test day is key to getting a high score. Familiarize yourself by looking online for some practice tests. Better yet, consider taking a TOEFL prep class with an experienced teacher.

#2: Study Academic English

Unlike some other English exams like the general IELTS test, the TOEFL is all about academic English. You may not have previously studied this kind of language before. Don't worry—that's what this book is all about!

#3: Practice Focusing for 2-3 Hours at a Time

This test takes a long time—around 2.5 hours for the paper-based one, and 3-4 hours for the computer one. Put your phone away and practice studying for a long period of time, without taking breaks. Get used to focusing for hours.

#4: Eat Breakfast and Get a Good Sleep

Make sure you're at your best for the exam. Get enough sleep the night before. It's a waste of time to "cram" and "pull an all-nighter!" It's best to be sharp and focused. Make sure to eat a good, healthy breakfast beforehand.

Bring a small snack to eat during the short breaks. Wear a t-shirt and bring a sweater along with you. This way, you can adapt to a hot or cold room and remain comfortable.

#5: Improve your English Typing Skills

You may be proficient at typing on a keyboard in your first language, but what about English? If you're doing the computer-based exam, this is a key factor. Make sure to do an online tutorial to improve your speed and accuracy.

If you're doing the paper based exam, be sure to bring sharpened pencils, an eraser, and a selection of nice pens.

#6: Practice Taking Notes

Note taking is a key skill for college students. It's also allowed on the TOEFL exam and can be helpful in getting a high score, so get some practice with it. Whenever you listen to, or read something, be sure to take some notes. Create your own shorthand for common words. For example, I use a triangle for "change." I also make frequent use of an equal sign, or an equal sign with a line through it to represent things like equal, similar, same, different, unequal, etc.

#7: Answer Every Single Question

On a multiple choice test with 4 questions, you have a 25% chance of randomly guessing the right answer. However, the good news is that there are usually 1 or 2 answers that are obviously not correct. Eliminate 1 of them, and you have a 33% chance. Eliminate 2, and you have a 50% chance of getting it right.

All that to say, never leave blanks on this exam. Answer every single question. Try to eliminate some answers, if possible, and then make your best guess. For the speaking portion, just say something. You may get partial points.

#8: Practice Writing with a Time Limit

Are you one of those people who carefully choose every word that you write in English? Maybe you ponder over whether or not your sentence is grammatically perfect? This is a bad habit that you need to break for the TOEFL exam. There is a strict time limit, and you won't finish the tasks if you do this.

Look up some writing practice tests for the TOEFL online. Follow the time limits. I recommend spending a short time thinking about the points you want to cover and making some brief notes about that (1-2 minutes per section). Then, start writing. Allow 3-5 minutes for proofreading at the end to check for any mistakes. Get used to doing this during your practice sessions, and you'll ace the exam.

#9: Make a Study Plan

You will have to spend a significant amount of time preparing for this exam if you want to get a high score. I don't want to lie about that! The best thing to do is to start around 6 months before. Make a study plan. Include a mix of all four skills, along with studying academic English vocabulary. Learn about the test format and do practice exams. When the test day comes, you'll be able to feel confident that you've put your best effort in!

#10: Choose a Test Date Wisely

Maybe you're doing the TOEFL to apply for a college or university? Don't plan to get your results only a few days before the college application deadline. What if your score isn't high enough? You won't have time to study more, retake the test, and wait for your results.

Instead, I recommend doing the first attempt 6-8 months before the application deadline. If you do well, that's great! If you don't, then you still have 3-4 more months to study, retake the test, and submit your application. This is the stress-free way!

This page intentionally left blank.

Brash and Aggressive

Kevin and Sandy are talking about one of Keith's classmates.

Sandy: How are your classes this semester?

Keith: Oh, they're fine, except for my political science class. There's one student that I **despise**.

Sandy: What does he do?

Keith: Well, he's so, **brusque**, **brash,** and **aggressive**. He'll say anything to anyone, and he **brags** about how much he knows. I'm certainly not **accustomed to** that.

Sandy: What does the professor do?

Keith: He doesn't **conceal** his dislike but not much besides that. I don't think he likes **conflict**. And this student is so **adamant** about what he thinks that I don't think anything the professor might say could change his mind.

Vocabulary

despite: Strong hate.

brusque: Abrupt to the point of rudeness.

brash: Rude, loud, in your face.

aggressive: Assertive or pushy.

brags: Boasts.

accustomed to: Used to something.

conceal: Hide.

conflict: Disagreement.

adamant: Refuse to change an opinion.

Vocabulary Challenge

1. Believe it or not, I don't _____ him. I know it's hard to understand.

2. If you beat your brother at a game, be a good winner and don't _____ about it.

3. I was sure she was lying but she was so _____ that she wasn't.

4. We need to _____ this. I don't want the media to get wind of it.

5. Keith and I have so much _____. I think we need to break up.

6. Play hard but don't be too _____, or nobody will want to play with you.

7. Toby is kind of _____, but everyone puts up with him because he's a hard worker.

8. Running is fine if you're _____ it. It's just difficult starting out.

Answers

1. despise

2. brag

3. adamant

4. conceal

5. conflict

6. aggressive

7. brash/brusque

8. accustomed to

Sam's Dissertation

Kerry and Tom are discussing Sam's dissertation.

Kerry*:* Did you see Sam's **dissertation**? He just **published** it.

Tom*:* I read the **abstract** and had a quick look at his **literature review**. What did you think?

Kerry: He certainly **cited** some less than **reputable sources** with no academic **credentials**.

Tom: I didn't notice that at first glance. Who's his **advisor**? I wonder how that slipped by him?

Kerry: Professor Brown. Sam must have **consulted** with him about his sources, right?

Tom: Who knows. Professor Brown has so much other stuff going on that he probably didn't read it. Isn't he going to retire next year too? He probably doesn't care. **The bottom line** is that nobody is going to take it seriously unless Sam **cleans up** this issue.

Vocabulary

dissertation: The final step in a Ph.D. Program; a written document with original research.

published: In the academic world, it refers to a research paper in a journal.

abstract: A summary of the thesis and primary ideas covered in an academic paper.

literature review: A summary of what other people have already written and published about a topic.

reputable sources: People who are experts in their fields and who have good reputations.

credentials: Qualifications. In this case, refers to academic degrees (at the graduate level), university titles, or publications.

advisor: Someone who offers assistance because of their higher level of knowledge. In an academic setting, it's usually a senior professor.

consulted: Talked with, usually for the purpose of getting expert or knowledgable advice.

the bottom line: What it comes down to in the end. The lowest or minimum standard.

cleans up: Corrects errors to make something look good.

Vocabulary Challenge

1. I think my _____ will take at least a year to complete.

2. Who are the _____ in this field? I don't have enough experience to know that yet.

3. I don't want to read this until she _____ all those spelling and simple grammar mistakes.

4. I only read the _____ of most papers if I'm short on time.

5. Has Tim _____ anything yet? Hasn't he been at this university for five years now?

6. You should have _____ with your advisor before you started writing your dissertation. She would have caught this mistake.

7. Start with a _____ before doing anything else on your thesis. You need to know what everyone else has already said.

8. _____ is that this isn't good enough for a Ph.D. student.

9. Do you that think my _____ are good enough to apply for an assistant professor job?

10. I'm thinking of asking Professor Bolen to be my _____.

Answers

1. dissertation
2. reputable sources
3. cleans up
4. abstract
5. published
6. consulted
7. literature review
8. the bottom line
9. credentials
10. advisor

Add insult to injury

Meaning: Make something already bad worse. For example, a guy fell off his bike but then a car ran over his foot.

Origin: Possibly from the ancient Roman fable of a bald man and a fly. The man tried to crush a fly on his head but used too much force and hurt himself too.

Example TOEFL question: Do you like your major?

Possible answer: It's fine, but there are some negatives. It's more difficult and time-consuming than a humanities or social science major because of all the required labs. This adds hours of class time each week. *To add insult to injury*, the labs are usually very early in the morning or late at night for freshman students.

A dime a dozen

Meaning: Something that is very common; not special.

Origin: First seen in the early 1800s when you could often buy a dozen (12) things for $0.10 (a dime).

Example TOEFL question: Is marketing a popular job in your country?

Possible answer: Yes, for sure. Marketing and PR people are *a dime a dozen* in all of Europe. It can be quite difficult for them to get jobs unless they have some sort of specialized skill like paid advertising.

A piece of cake

Meaning: Something that's easy to do.

Origin: From the 1870s. Cakes were often given as prizes during competitions and at fairs, so that's why they're associated with something being easy to do.

Example TOEFL question: Why did you choose your field of study?

Possible answer: Honestly, I'm a little bit of a lazy student, and my friend told me that this course was *a piece of cake* but would lead to a well-paying job. It's not as easy as she said, but it's still not that difficult and most people get jobs quite easily after they graduate.

A tough pill to swallow (A bitter pill to swallow)

Meaning: Something difficult to get over or accept.

Origin: First seen in the 1600s. Probably related to medicine pills that can be big or bitter when you have to swallow them.

Example TOEFL question: Describe an unexpected event.

Possible answer: I remember when I took the road test for my driver's license for the first time, and I failed. I was very confident in my abilities, so it was *a tough pill to swallow*. But, looking back on it, the examiner was correct in that I wasn't a safe driver at that time!

Beat around the bush

Meaning: Avoid talking about something important, or not getting to the main point directly.

Origin: From the early 1400s. Rich men used to hire people to beat the bushes when they went hunting to scare the birds out of them so that they could shoot them.

Example TOEFL question: Do you get along well with your classmates?

Possible answer: Generally yes, except for one of them. She is famous for *beating around the bush* and talking way too much during class. I think she just likes hearing her own voice! It's quite annoying.

Widespread Abuse

Tammy is talking to Cindy about a policy at her work.

Cindy: How's that new unlimited sick day policy at your work going? Did your company **proceed** with it?

Tammy: Oh, it's ridiculous. There's **widespread** abuse. Most people are taking every Friday or Monday off and getting paid for it. When they implemented it, it was **obvious** that it was never going to work.

Cindy: What happens if you get caught abusing it?

Tammy: That's the thing. Nothing. That's the **core** issue. My company is far too **lenient** on the lazy people. There was no **strategy** to encourage people to show up every day. Human resources is basically **incompetent**.

Cindy: So what's going to happen?

Tammy: Well, productivity is way down. They'll have to **suspend** it, I think.

Vocabulary

proceed: Start or continue with something.

widespread: Describes something that occurs widely, over a large area or time.

obvious: Easily understood.

core: Central, of main importance.

lenient: Not harsh; merciful.

strategy: A plan to reach a desired outcome.

incompetent: Incapable.

suspend: Stop, usually temporarily.

Vocabulary Challenge

1. There's _____ cheating in his class. He just reads a book during tests.

2. My boss is totally _____. I'm sure she'll get fired soon.

3. We need to _____ your daughter for a week. You can't hit other kids at school.

4. My husband says I'm too _____ with the kids. He might be right.

5. Let's _____ with the sale.

6. The solution is _____ to me. We need to fire Toni.

7. What's the _____ issue here? We keep beating around the bush.

8. What's our _____ here? Should we price it high or low?

Answers

1. widespread

2. incompetent

3. suspend

4. lenient

5. proceed

6. obvious

7. core

8. strategy

Ample Time

Ethan is talking to his professor after class about his assignment.

Ethan: Hi, I'd like to follow up about those emails I sent you. I asked if I could get an **extension** on that assignment. But, you didn't email back.

Professor: I didn't email back because I've been very clear. There are no extensions in my classes. You had **ample** time—I told you about the assignment more than a month ago. You can't **deny** that you had enough time if you were organized.

Ethan: Yes, but I have a midterm exam in another class this week too.

Professor: That's the life of a student, isn't it? I know that my policy may seem **harsh** but is your future boss going to be kind if you keep missing deadlines? I've never **misled** anyone about my policy. I've stated it at least 10 times.

Ethan: Who else can I talk to about this? Who is your boss?

Professor: You will not **coerce** me, or my boss into giving you an extension. I recommend that you don't **persist** with this. It will get you nothing. Focus your time and attention on your assignment! You still have one more day. That's an **adequate** amount of time.

Vocabulary

extension: The act of making something longer.

ample: Plentiful; enough.

deny: State that something isn't true.

harsh: Not gentle.

misled: Gave the wrong idea about something.

coerce: Force someone to do something that they don't want to do.

persist: Continuing with something, especially when facing opposition.

adequate: Enough to suit your needs.

Vocabulary Challenge

1. Do you think Professor Bolen will give me an _____? My grandmother is in the hospital.

2. The contractors _____ about how much the final cost would be.

3. You have _____ time to finish your homework before soccer practice. If you don't finish, you won't be able to go to soccer.

4. My salary is _____, but not enough for luxuries.

5. Stop trying to _____ me. I'm not going to do it.

6. You can't _____ that I'm better at managing finances.

7. It's a bit _____, but I think we should take away Toni's computer for a week. What she did was so bad.

8. If you _____ in asking me, I'm just going to get angry.

Answers

1. extension
2. misled
3. ample
4. adequate
5. coerce
6. deny
7. harsh
8. persist

Beef Up

Tim and Nathan are talking about cybersecurity at their company.

Tim: I think we need to **beef up** our cybersecurity. We're starting to **fall behind,** and I'm nervous we might **end up** getting hacked.

Nathan: I agree. It's time to **break out** all the tools. I'd rather do some prevention now if it means we don't have to **fight back** against some unknown enemy later.

Tim: I agree. Let's **get it over with**. We have to do it at some point and better late than never.

Nathan: For sure. But, we can't get **carried away** with it. We still have to **stay within** the budget. Let's **hit up** Tony and see what he thinks about this. He's the head of security here.

Vocabulary

beef up: Increase.

fall behind: Not keep up with others.

end up: To be in a place that was not planned for in the end.

break out: Deploy or start to use something.

fight back: Counterattack in a fight or battle.

get it over with: Do something that you don't want to do.

carried away: Do something to an excessive degree.

stay within: Not go over budget or time; not exceed some limit.

hit up: Ask someone for something, usually a favour.

Vocabulary Challenge

1. We need to _____ the schedule time for this meeting. I have a dentist appointment after it.

2. I don't want to _____ being stuck next to him at lunch.

3. We're starting to _____ on this project. Let's stay late tonight and tomorrow and try to get back on track.

4. Let's _____ against Tim about this decision. It's clearly the wrong one for our company.

5. My kids always get _____ with games and never clean up!

6. Let's _____ your parents and see if they'll take us out for dinner tonight.

7. Let's _____ that wine you made. I think it's ready.

8. Cleaning the garage this weekend? I don't want to but let's _____.

9. Let's _____ our home security system. There have been a lot of break-ins recently.

Answers

1. stay within

2. end up

3. fall behind

4. fight back

5. carried away

6. hit up

7. break out

8. get it over with

9. beef up

Vanished Into Thin Air

Amy and Chloe are talking about some criminal activity in their city.

Amy: Do you remember the story of that 2-year old boy who **vanished** into thin air?

Chloe: It was all over the news. I heard that he showed up at his mom's house in the middle of the night after 2 weeks, apparently **unscathed**.

Amy: It was the strangest thing. I heard that the police barely **investigated** it. They just assumed his dad took him. But there was no **evidence** of that at all.

Chloe: The investigation did seem rather **haphazard**.

Amy: They are pretty much **negligent**. Thankfully he's okay. I think we need to **reinforce** our policing system with some more officers.

Chloe: I'm not sure that's the answer. I think we need to **reform** the policing system and get rid of the **corrupt** people at the top.

Vocabulary

vanished: Disappeared quickly.

unscathed: Unharmed.

investigated: Looked into; examined.

evidence: Facts or information to prove or disprove something.

haphazard: Not carefully; lacking planning.

negligent: Lazy; neglectful.

reinforce: Make something stronger.

reform: Makes changes to improve a situation.

corrupt: A willingness to act dishonestly.

Vocabulary Challenge

1. My keys seem to have _____. Will you help me look for them?

2. We need to _____ the management structure of our company.

3. I'm taking my doctor to court. I think he was _____.

4. You can go to war with your boss, but you won't escape _____.

5. Clean your room, but not in the _____ way you usually do it.

6. We need to _____ this fence, or it'll fall down.

7. I've _____ the matter, and I don't think Cindy did anything wrong.

8. Don't you think that all politicians are basically _____?

9. There's no _____ that she's been treating you unfairly. A feeling isn't enough.

Answers

1. vanished

2. reform

3. negligent

4. unscathed

5. haphazard

6. reinforce

7. investigated

8. corrupt

9. evidence

Hard to Decipher

Sam is talking to her professor about her research paper.

Professor: I've read your paper and have a few comments about it. You write **eloquently**, but it's hard to **decipher** what you're actually saying. There are a lot of **frivolous** words.

Sam: Oh no! I wanted to make it a bit **ambiguous**. It's a complicated issue.

Professor: That's not ideal for a research paper. You need to write **accurately** and **concisely**. You need to **emphasize** the key points.

Sam: Okay. That **clarifies** things. Thanks for your help.

Vocabulary

eloquently: With feeling or style. Refers to speaking or writing.

decipher: Find the meaning of.

frivolous: Unnecessary.

ambiguous: Not clear.

accurately: Correctly.

concisely: Brief, but contains all the required information.

emphasize: Give special importance.

clarifies: Makes clear.

Vocabulary Challenge

1. President Obama speaks so _____.

2. Let me do it. You need to copy down the details _____.

3. The additional information _____ things a little bit, but I'm still kind of confused.

4. What's your main point? You need to _____ it more strongly.

5. Your handwriting is so hard to _____.

6. I'm not sure if I'll get promoted or not. My performance reviews are kind of _____.

7. We need to cut down on our _____ spending.

8. Please write _____. The limit is 1000 words.

Answers

1. eloquently

2. accurately

3. clarifies

4. emphasize

5. decipher

6. ambiguous

7. frivolous

8. concisely

In the Ballpark

Keith is talking to his professor about his project.

Professor: I have some good news and some bad news. Which do you want to hear first?

Keith: I'll take the good news first, please.

Professor: Okay, well, you're **in the ballpark** in terms of **results**. But the bad news is that you'll have to get back in the **lab** to find more **precise** results.

Keith: They're not good enough to publish?

Professor: Not really. You'll have to **investigate** the exact reaction point more closely. I recommend using **trial and error** with some common agents. I know that repeating the same action over and over again with only small changes can be kind of **dull,** but it's important. Why don't you get Kevin to **assist** you? He's looking to get some **experience** in the lab.

Keith: Okay, I'll check with him. Thanks for your help.

Vocabulary

in the ballpark: Something is close to the desired outcome or target.

results: Outcome of something.

lab: Laboratory for doing science.

precise: Exact.

investigate: Look into.

trial and error: Doing something many times until you find what works best.

dull: Boring.

assist: Help.

experience: Knowledge gained through practice.

Vocabulary Challenge

1. I need to book some _____ time. Where's the sign-up sheet?

2. I've learned a lot about growing things under various light conditions through _____ in the lab.

3. You're _____ but not quite there yet.

4. I want to get some _____ in the business world to go along with my degree.

5. I find lab work so _____! You have to be so exact with your measurements.

6. Please find the _____ temperature at which it happens.

7. What do you plan to _____ for your dissertation?

8. Do you want someone to _____ you? I think Tony has some time.

9. What did the _____ show? Will that substance work as a reaction agent?

Answers

1. lab

2. trial and error

3. in the ballpark

4. experience

5. dull

6. precise

7. investigate

8. assist

9. results

Chronological Order

Jake is talking to his professor about a paper he has to write.

Jake: I'm really struggling with how to **decipher** the **copious** amounts of **data** on this subject. It seems like an **arduous** task. I kind of regret choosing this topic.

Professor: It's an interesting topic. Don't give up on it.

Jake: So can I organize things?

Professor: Well, you'll need to **aggregate** it in an organized fashion. My **inclination** would be to organize it in **chronological** order and perhaps group it into 5 or 10-year periods. This will make it more manageable.

Jake: That seems **feasible**. I never thought about doing it that way. I appreciate your help.

Professor: No problem. Come see me next week, and I'll take a quick look at it.

Vocabulary

decipher: Find the meaning of.

copious: Abundant.

data: Facts, evidence.

arduous: Requiring a lot of effort.

aggregate: Combine.

inclination: Preference; tendency.

chronological: Arranged in order by date or time.

feasible: Possible to do.

Vocabulary Challenge

1. What does this say? His handwriting is so hard to _____.

2. Please organize it in _____ fashion.

3. Isn't there an app or something that can _____ all this data for us?

4. We have _____ amounts of food! Don't worry.

5. My _____ is to go camping this summer, instead of flying somewhere.

6. I know that you think you're right, but the _____ says otherwise.

7. It's not _____ for us to hire someone else. You'll just have to work harder.

8. The hike was _____. I was so exhausted afterwards.

Answers

1. decipher

2. chronological

3. aggregate

4. copious

5. inclination

6. data

7. feasible

8. arduous

Rigid Thinking

Cara is talking to her coworker Sandra about Bob (another coworker)

Sandra: You look troubled. What's up?

Cara: You know Bob, right? He's looking for a promotion and asked me to **recommend** him.

Sandra: You **supervise** him, right? What's the issue?

Cara: Well, only **briefly**. In my time with him, he's not a good employee. He's so **rigid** in this thinking. He's not a **desirable** candidate for that job.

Sandra: Really? He always seems so **upbeat** when I bump into him.

Cara: He is. That's the tricky part. He's a genuinely nice guy, but he's not open to **feedback.** I don't want to **distort** that fact about him or **deceive** anyone.

Sandra: I get that. If you give him a positive recommendation and he does poorly at his new job, it will make you look bad.

Cara: Yes. Exactly. I'm hoping to **evade** the issue as long as possible.

Vocabulary

recommend: Put forward something or someone for approval.

supervise: Oversee.

briefly: For a short amount of time.

rigid: Unyielding; not flexible.

desirable: Worth having.

upbeat: Happy, positive.

distort: Misrepresent.

deceive: Trick or mislead.

evade: Avoid.

Vocabulary Challenge

1. I honestly can't _____ him for the job.

2. Well, he's not outright lying but he did _____ the truth. I can't trust him.

3. I'm wondering if you'll _____ me for my comprehensive exams?

4. I try to be _____ most of the time.

5. You can't _____ me all night! We have to talk about your poor grades.

6. I don't like it when you _____ me about where you are.

7. I _____ dated a famous basketball player!

8. My husband is very _____ about how much sleep he gets.

9. The _____ option is Ted Jones, but I'm sure he'll get a better offer at another company.

Answers

1. recommend

2. distort

3. supervise

4. upbeat

5. evade

6. deceive

7. briefly

8. rigid

9. desirable

Confusing Words: Accept/Except

Listening/pronunciation tip: These two words only have a slight difference in pronunciation which makes them confusing. Focus on the first vowel sound of each word. "Accept" has a sharp and short "a" like in "apple," whereas the first sound of "except" has an "e" like in "egg."

accept: A verb that means to take or receive something (willingly, with permission). It can also mean to believe or recognize an opinion, story, or theory.

Most people accept that the theory of evolution is true.

I accepted the job offer. I'll start in two weeks.

His parents accepted his decision to not go to college.

I can't accept his apology. What he did was just so bad.

except: Used as a preposition to mean not including or other than; not included, something not a part of a grouping. Also used as a verb but not commonly (usually in legal documents).

That restaurant is open every day except for Mondays.

The letter is great except for one thing—there are a few spelling mistakes. Use spell check on your computer.

He does nothing except complain. I'm so tired of it.

I have to work every day except for Tuesdays.

Vocabulary Challenge

1. Are you going to _____ the revised contract?

2. That house is good, _____ it only has one bathroom.

3. We're open for lunch, _____ on Tuesdays.

4. Can you _____ my package for me, please? It's going to be delivered on my day off.

5. Please _____ my sincere apology.

6. He's a great employee _____ he always shows up a few minutes late.

Answers

1. accept

2. except

3. except

4. accept

5. accept

6. except

Speaking practice: After checking your fill-in-the-blank answers, try speaking each sentence to a friend. Or, record yourself speaking each sentence on your smartphone. Then listen and see if your pronunciation is clear and easy to understand.

What's the Verdict?

Kevin and Bob are talking about whether or not to hire Ken.

Kevin: So, what's the **verdict**? Are we going to hire Ken?

Bob: I keep **vacillating**! We do have a **sufficient** number of people, but he does have some **expertise** on that new machine we just bought. What do you think?

Kevin: It's **likely** that we'll run into problems with that machine at some point. Do we have anyone who knows how to fix it?

Bob: Not right now. Hmmm . . . I actually **detect** a future problem here!

Kevin: Well, we will **require** someone eventually. We should go for it. The worst thing for a company to do is to remain **stagnant**. We need to keep growing, and Ken is an excellent choice.

Vocabulary

verdict: Judgement or decision.

vacillating: Wavering.

sufficient: Enough for a particular purpose.

expertise: Expert level knowledge about a certain thing.

likely: Probable.

detect: Locate something.

require: Need.

stagnant: Slugging, not changing or growing.

Vocabulary Challenge

1. What was the _____ in that murder trial that was in the news?

2. To finish the paperwork, I _____ a copy of your passport.

3. Do I _____ a hint of sarcasm? Just tell me how you really feel about it.

4. I'm _____ between Greece or Thailand for vacation.

5. I _____ won't make it for beers. I have to finish this report up.

6. You have a _____ amount of research. It's time to start writing your report.

7. Talk to Emma. She has some _____ in this area.

8. My company is _____. Nothing ever changes.

Answers

1. verdict

2. require

3. detect

4. vacillating

5. likely

6. sufficient

7. expertise

8. stagnant

A Dilemma

Kevin and Tracy are talking about a situation at work.

Tracy: How are things going with your team?

Kevin: Not great. We keep missing deadlines and getting work sent back because it's not high enough quality. I don't know how to **mend** things. It's a real **dilemma**. As their **intrepid** leader, I feel like I've failed. I've tried to **evaluate** what's going on, but I'm not sure.

Tracy: Well, team **cohesion** is key. The **fundamental flaw** of your team seems to be a lack of team spirit. You need to be **cognizant** of the relationships between people.

Kevin: I'm terrible at that. That must be why we're struggling.

Tracy: Focus on creating a positive atmosphere. **Praise** goes a long way too!

Kevin: I'm happy that I talked to you about this.

Vocabulary

mend: To fix.

dilemma: A Situation requiring a difficult choice.

intrepid: Fearless.

evaluate: Assess.

cohesion: Uniting, or becoming one.

fundamental: Basic; of primary importance.

flaw: A feature that ruins the perfection of something.

cognizant: Being aware of something.

praise: To give approval or admiration.

Vocabulary Challenge

1. Do you think we can _____ that zipper instead of throwing it out?

2. _____ is key to any team.

3. I have a _____. I said that I'd be in two places at the same time!

4. Please be _____ of that fact that I'm terribly out of shape! You'll have to walk a bit slower.

5. The _____ problem is that we have a hard time talking to each other.

6. Let's _____ what went wrong here.

7. A bit of _____ goes a long way! Tell people when they do a good job of something.

8. You're such an _____ traveler! I can't believe you did that by yourself.

9. It looks great. The only _____ is that you didn't cite your references in the correct format.

Answers

1. mend

2. cohesion

3. dilemma

4. cognizant

5. fundamental

6. evaluate

7. praise

8. intrepid

9. flaw

Lab Homework

A professor is talking to her students about a lab report that they have to do.

I want to talk a little bit about your upcoming **lab report**. Remember that it's **due** next Thursday at the beginning of class. I won't accept late assignments.

The most important thing is to **analyze** the reactions of the compound at different temperatures. Once you get some **results**, please **validate** them somehow. How you do this is up to you, but you'll have to explain why you chose that in your lab report. Remember that **technique** is very important here if you want to **replicate** your results, so pay close attention.

In your report, be sure to **cite your references** clearly in the **footnotes**. I expect you to use at least three sources. Your **TA** will be available between now and next Thursday if you have any questions.

Vocabulary

lab report: A paper written that talks about results from an experiment.

due: Expected at a certain time.

analyze: Examine something closely.

results: Outcome of something.

validate: Confirm research testing is correct; test research results in order to show work is accurate.

technique: How to do something.

replicate: Do something using the exact same process to get the same results.

cite your references: Say where you're getting information from.

footnotes: At the bottom of the page in a lab report, thesis, or paper. Contains extra information.

TA: Teaching assistant (usually a graduate student) who helps a professor teach students.

Vocabulary Challenge

1. Can I see your _____? I got such a bad grade on mine, but I'm not sure what went wrong.

2. I can't seem to _____ my initial findings. Can you help me figure out what's happening?

3. Okay, now you should _____ your findings. Do the experiment one more time and make sure you find the same thing.

4. When is the report _____?

5. Be sure to _____ in the _____. You can get in big trouble if you don't.

6. Can you _____ this data and then write a report for me, please?

7. She has excellent _____ for adjusting slides under the microscope. Please watch her.

8. I'm going to be a _____ for Professor Bolen next year.

9. The _____ don't seem right. I expected the opposite to happen. Let's do the experiment again.

Answers

1. lab report
2. replicate
3. validate
4. due
5. cite your references, footnotes
6. analyze
7. technique
8. TA
9. results

Advocate for Yourself

Min-Gyu is talking to his friend Jae-Hun about one of his professors.

Jae-Hun: You look down. What's going on?

Min-Gyu: I keep getting **overlooked** when it comes to co-authoring papers. My professor thinks I'm useless just because English isn't my first language.

Jae-Hun: You have **exemplary** English. You need to **advocate** for yourself and not let him **diminish** you. **Boost** your image. Have you tried talking to him about it?

Min-Gyu: No. Maybe I should. I'm scared of an **adverse** response, I guess.

Jae-Hun: Well, **devise** a plan. Write down some talking points. Show him that you deserve more respect than he's giving him.

Min-Gyu: Yes, I **concur** with everything you're saying! I'm happy that I talked to you about it.

Jae-Hun: That's what friends are for.

Vocabulary

overlooked: Failed to notice something or someone.

exemplary: Outstanding.

advocate: Speak or write in support of.

diminish: Shrink or reduce in some way.

boost: Raise.

adverse: Unfavorable or difficult positions.

devise: Plan, create.

concur: Agree.

Vocabulary Challenge

1. I think we've _____ something here. Why don't the numbers add up?

2. You did well under some _____ conditions.

3. I don't want to _____ his achievements, but I think he got most of them by cheating.

4. She's an _____ tennis player.

5. I _____. However, there are a couple of small things that I don't agree with.

6. I'm wondering how we can _____ our social media presence?

7. I want to _____ for myself more at work. I always get the worst tasks because I have a difficult time saying no.

8. Let's _____ a plan for getting you that promotion that you want!

Answers

1. overlooked

2. adverse

3. diminish

4. exemplary

5. concur

6. boost

7. advocate

8. devise

Noise Pollution

Kathleen is asking Kenny about Busan.

Kathleen: Kenny! You lived in Busan, South Korea? I've always wanted to go there. What's it like? I've heard that it's a beautiful **coastal city**.

Kenny: Well, there's a lot **light pollution**. It's the second biggest city in Korea. And **traffic jams** too during **rush hour**.

Kathleen: It sounds terrible.

Kenny: Oh no, it's amazing! I love Nampo-Dong, which has lots of **street food** and **street vendors,** plus **trendy cafes**. It's perfect for a date.

Kathleen: What else?

Kenny: Well, there's no real **downtown core** or **main square,** but there are six beaches within **city limits**. Most people just **hang out** there, especially in the summertime.

Vocabulary

coastal city: A city next to the ocean.

light pollution: Light from signs and cars that you can see inside your house at night.

traffic jams: Lots of cars on the road which makes progress slower than normal.

rush hour: The busiest times to drive, usually in the morning and after work.

street food: Food from an outside stall.

street vendors: People selling things at an outside stall.

trendy cafes: Coffee shops that are fashionable and hip.

downtown core: The area in a city with lots of tall buildings; an important place of business.

main square: The most important public courtyard in a city.

city limits: The entire city, including suburbs. Not just the downtown core.

hang out: Spend time together.

Vocabulary Challenge

1. Do you want to _____ tonight?

2. I love to buy Christmas presents from _____. There are lots of interesting things.

3. Vancouver is the best _____ in Canada.

4. Within the _____, you can find three beaches and countless parks.

5. Go after 9:30 am to avoid _____.

6. Where's the _____? I'd love to spend some time there and people watch.

7. The best _____ in Korea? Honestly, I can't choose. There are many delicious things.

8. The _____ in Edmonton is famous for being boring at night.

9. _____ makes it difficult for me to sleep at night even though I have blackout curtains.

10. My boyfriend loves to spend time at _____ on weekends. I think they're expensive!

11. During _____, it takes twice as long to get home.

Answers

1. hang out

2. street vendors

3. coastal city

4. city limits

5. traffic jams

6. main square

7. street food

8. downtown core

9. light pollution

10. trendy cafes

11. rush hour

Shades of Gray

Terry and Sandra are Biology classmates discussing the issue of cloning.

Terry: What did you think about the **lecture** today? Interesting, right?

Sandra: The lecture raised a lot of ethical questions for me about **cloning**. It's not a **black and white** issue. There are so many **shades of gray**.

Terry: Definitely. There should be way stricter standards for replicating living things. At the end of the day, it shouldn't only come down to the researcher's **values** and **ethics**.

Sandra: Yes, **it goes without saying**. But who will **develop** these standards? Universities? **Industry**? The government?

Terry: That **remains to be seen**. Likely it'll be a combination of those things. Cloning is still a very new thing. And that's to say nothing of AI. But, I **digress**.

Vocabulary

lecture: In a university or college, where a professor gives information by talking about it. Typically, a 2-3 hour class that is held once a week.

cloning: Making a copy of something.

black and white: There *is* a clear right and wrong.

shades of gray: There *is no* clear right and wrong.

values: Basic, fundamental beliefs about something.

ethics: Moral principles that govern a person's behavior or the conducting of an activity.

it goes without saying: It's obvious.

develop: Make something new.

industry: For-profit companies.

remains to be seen: The outcome of something is undecided at the current time.

digress: Wander from the subject at hand.

Vocabulary Challenge

1. That _____ was so boring. I think I fell asleep for a few minutes.

2. That company has so many issues I think because they have no core _____.

3. It's a difficult situation! There are no _____ answers here.

4. Do you think that in 100 years from now, _____ of humans will be possible?

5. The university is putting together a committee to _____ some guidelines about cloning.

6. Sorry to _____, but what about Tina? We'll need to fire her too.

7. I can't tell you what to do in this situation. It depends on your personal _____.

8. You can make more money in _____ jobs than with the government but the benefits aren't as good.

9. It _____ whether or not I'll pass that test. It was so difficult.

10. _____ that he's the best choice for an advisor, but he already has so many students.

11. I enjoy studying bioethics but I don't like that there are so many _____ for almost everything.

Answers

1. lecture

2. values

3. black and white

4. cloning

5. develop

6. digress

7. ethics/values

8. industry

9. remains to be seen

10. it goes without saying

11. shades of gray

Behind the scenes

Meaning: What happens out of sight from the public.

Origin: Refers to backstage at a performance of some kind. It's what the audience can't see.

Example TOEFL question: What do you think of fast food?

Possible answer: Well, at face value, it's quite cheap, tastes good, and is convenient. However, there's a lot going on *behind the scenes* with regard to animal cruelty and low wages for employees, so I generally try to avoid it.

Better late than never

Meaning: Encouragement after getting a late start to something.

Origin: First seen in 1396 in the *Canterbury Tales*.

Example TOEFL question: How has the education system changed in your country in the past few decades?

Possible answer: One big change is that corporal punishment is now banned. It should have happened a long time ago, but *better late than never*.

Break the bank

Meaning: Something that costs a lot or more than you can afford.

Origin: From the 1600s. Referred to gamblers winning more than the house (referred to as a bank) could afford.

Example TOEFL question: How can the government help unemployed people?

Possible answer: I think there could be way more training programs for unemployed people. It wouldn't *break the bank,* and it would benefit employers to have more highly skilled workers, particularly in the trades or technical areas.

Burning the midnight oil

Meaning: Working very long hours, late into the night.

Origin: First seen in the 1600s. Candles and oil were used to provide light before electricity, so refers to someone working late into the night.

Example TOEFL question: Are you a good student?

Possible answer: I study way too much, particularly around the midterm and final exam periods. Students have to *burn the midnight oil* pretty much all of December and April!

Burn the candle at both ends

Meaning: Work very hard from early morning to late at night.

Origin: The early meaning of this idiom was to be frugal. Candles were expensive, so if you wanted to save money, you'd burn both ends. Later, it was used to refer to working too hard, possibly burning the first end of the candle but wanting to continue work so burning the other end too.

Example TOEFL question: Do you like your subject at college?

Possible answer: Yes, it's not bad, but there are a lot of group projects that take up so much time. Combined with my part-time job, I find that I'm *burning the candle at both ends* most weeks.

Dry Up

Karen and Ellie are talking about finding a job.

Karen: All my contacts seem to have **dried up.** Have you heard of any work?

Ellie: What about that job you **applied for**? Did you **follow up** with them?

Karen: Their funding **fell through** in the end, and they didn't hire anyone.

Ellie: Oh, I didn't know about that. Do you want to **stick with** this industry, or are you **open to** other possibilities? You might be able to **fill in** for a position at my company. Someone is going on maternity leave.

Karen: I'd **settle for** just about anything. I'm about to **give up**.

Vocabulary

dried up: Ran out.

applied for: Sent in a job application.

follow up: Contact someone you've talked to previously about a job, business deal, etc.

fell through: Didn't work out.

stick with: Stay with the same thing.

open to: Willing to consider it.

fill in: Replace temporarily.

settle for: Accept something not ideal.

give up: Stop trying.

Vocabulary Challenge

1. Don't _____, okay? Things will get better.

2. If you _____ this, you'll get some good results.

3. Please _____ for me when I'm on vacation.

4. My job offer _____ when we couldn't agree on vacation time.

5. I don't want to _____ the first job offer I get. I have lots of valuable skills.

6. It'd be better if you were _____ working for Tommy as well.

7. The funding has _____, and we'll have to shut this project down.

8. Please _____ with me next week, okay?

9. I _____ ten jobs and only heard back from one of them.

Answers

1. give up

2. stick with

3. fill in

4. fell through

5. settle for

6. open to

7. dried up

8. follow up

9. applied for

Confusing Words: Adverse/Averse

Both of these words indicate difficult (sometimes dangerous) conditions that make success or development hard. Both words sound similar.

Listening/pronunciation tip: Listen for the "d" sound to distinguish between the two words. You can also listen for where the syllable stress is placed:

- AD-verse has the first syllable stressed, the second is soft/weak

- a-VERSE has the emphasis stressed on the second part of the word, "-verse"

adverse: An adjective that usually relates to things and means harmful or unfavourable conditions for an action or person/people/animals, etc. "Adversity" is the noun form.

Approving this development will have an adverse impact on the animals that live there.

People are going to have an adverse reaction to him keeping his job. We need to fire him.

You may have some adverse side effects with this medication.

I overcame a lot of adversity to finally finish college.

averse: An adjective that usually applies to people and means a feeling or distaste or dislike; opposition to something. "Aversion" is the noun form.

My son is averse to eating vegetables of any kind.

I'm not averse to hiring another person, but you'll have to show me the numbers.

I think my kids are averse to doing the dishes. I have to threaten them to do it.

I have a strong aversion to doing laundry!

Vocabulary Challenge

1. Did you experience any _____ effects from the vaccine?

2. Honestly, I'm _____ to kids. It's not my idea of fun to go on vacation with them.

3. I have an _____ to work.

4. My boss is _____ to people coming early and leaving early. We all stick to the 9-5.

5. I'm worried about the _____ impact that lots of mandatory overtime will have on employee morale.

6. I experienced a lot of _____ when I decided to go back to work as a single mom. It was so difficult.

Answers

1. adverse

2. averse

3. aversion

4. averse

5. adverse

6. adversity

Speaking practice: After checking your fill-in-the-blank answers, try speaking each sentence to a friend. Or, record yourself speaking each sentence on your smartphone. Then listen and see if your pronunciation is clear and easy to understand.

Scrutinize Carefully

Bob is talking to his classmate Toby about changing colleges.

Bob: Hey Toby, so I'm thinking about **transferring** to ABC college to finish my degree.

Toby: Oh wow! That seems like a **hasty** decision. Why?

Bob: I've been thinking about it for a while. My **primary** concern with this place is the huge class sizes. I don't even know my professors.

Toby: True, but it's so **prestigious**. You'll have to **scrutinize** ABC carefully. What is a degree from there actually worth? And don't **assume** you'll have smaller class sizes. You might not.

Bob: You make valid points.

Toby: Personally, I'm wiling to **tolerate** a lot at this place to get a degree from here. It'll be so easy to get a job when I graduate because of it.

Vocabulary

transferring: Moving from one place to another one.

hasty: In a hurry.

primary: First.

prestigious: Having a good reputation.

scrutinize: Examine carefully.

assume: Think something, without proof.

tolerate: Put up with something.

Vocabulary Challenge

1. I can't believe you're _____. I'll be sad to see you go.

2. We need to _____ this deal carefully. That company doesn't have a good reputation.

3. Let's not make a _____ decision. It's too important.

4. We can safely _____ that he won't be here next week!

5. The _____ concern I have is that she shows up late every day.

6. Honestly, I can _____ a lot if they get the work done, but not this.

7. I want to go to a _____ university after I graduate from high school.

Answers

1. transferring

2. scrutinize

3. hasty

4. assume

5. primary

6. tolerate

7. prestigious

Writing Homework

A professor is talking to her students about an essay that they have to write for homework.

You have to write an **essay** on a **controversial** topic that has two distinct sides. For example, whether or not a country should allow abortion. Choose which side to defend and then write a **thesis statement**. Put it in the first **paragraph**, the introduction.

Then, write 3-4 body paragraphs, depending on how many reasons you'll include. Each paragraph should start with a good **topic sentence**. Remember that a topic sentence is a supporting reason for your thesis. Include some **persuasive** evidence or facts to support your **opinion**. Defend it well!

Finally, write a good conclusion where you briefly **summarize** what your opinion is and some of the key points of **evidence**. You can submit the first draft to me **via** email.

Vocabulary

essay: A short piece of writing about a certain subject or topic.

controversial: Something causing disagreement that has different, strong opinions about it.

thesis statement: The most important sentence in an essay—it tells people what they will read about and is the opinion of the writer.

paragraph: Several sentences (usually 4-10) about one topic.

topic sentence: The most important sentence in a paragraph—it tells people what the paragraph is about. In an opinion essay, it's a reason to support the thesis statement.

persuasive: Convincing. In this case, it's a kind of essay that tries to persuade the reader to change their opinion about the topic using reason.

opinion: A belief, view, or judgement about something, not always based on knowledge/facts.

summarize: Briefly state the most important points about something.

evidence: Facts or information that show something to be true or right.

via: By; through.

Vocabulary Challenge

1. When is that _____ due? Next Friday, right? I think it has to be 5 or 6 _____.

2. You'll need to do some research to find some solid _____.

3. Please circle the _____ and _____. I want to see them clearly.

4. You only need to _____ the article. It should be a maximum of four sentences.

5. Did you find him to be _____? I don't think he made any good points at all.

6. Please send your application _____ email or physical mail. It doesn't matter to me.

7. In the USA, climate change is a _____ subject. In most parts of the world, it's not.

8. I want to see lots of solid facts, reasons, and examples. It should be more than just your _____.

Answers

1. essay, paragraphs

2. evidence

3. thesis statement/topic sentences

4. summarize

5. persuasive

6. via

7. controversial

8. opinion

A Few Qualms

Toby and Kay are talking about a presentation they have to do for a class.

Toby: Kay, what are you thinking about for our presentation? We have to pick something controversial and **argue** one side of it, right?

Kay: Yes. My **instinct** is always to choose something **wildly** unpopular and argue it in an **over the top** kind of way, just for fun. Maybe something along the lines of how Sweden's approach to Covid-19 was better than countries that went into full **lockdown**?

Toby: Oh, interesting. That's not without **risk** though. I do have a few **qualms** about how our professor will **perceive** it, but it would be interesting to look into the stats for that.

Kay: Oh, I expect some **outrage** for sure! But, you only live once, right?

Toby: We have to be careful to not get a low grade though. My parents will kill me.

Kay: I'll never tell! Let's keep talking via text. I'd love to get something **set in stone** by tonight.

Vocabulary

argue: Talk angrily or loudly about opposing views about something.

instinct: An unlearned behaviour that happens in response to something else.

wildly: Extreme, uncontrolled, or severe.

over the top: Excessive; exaggerated.

lockdown: In this case, relates to Covid-19 where people have to stay at home.

risk: A situation that involves potential danger.

qualms: Hesitations.

perceive: Understand.

outrage: Anger over something unjust, unfair, or wrong. Can sometimes be an overreaction to something that is not based on logic.

set in stone: Something permanent and not able to be changed.

Vocabulary Challenge

1. I do have a few _____ about recommending Sarah for that assistant professor position.

2. Did you see that press conference! I have so much _____ that I don't even know what to do with it.

3. My _____ is to just pretend that I didn't see him do that.

4. Each group will _____ one side during the debate. Now, let's choose groups and sides.

5. The final exam date isn't _____ yet. I'll let you know as soon as I find out.

6. It's a big _____ but I'm going to change jobs.

7. During _____, I watched more TV than I ever have in my life.

8. The most important thing is how you _____ yourself.

9. Don't you find Professor Bolen a bit _____? She is always so happy about everything.

10. Professor Brown is _____ popular. His classes fill up in minutes.

Answers

1. qualms
2. outrage
3. instinct
4. argue
5. set in stone
6. risk
7. lockdown
8. perceive
9. over the top
10. wildly

Applying for University

John is talking to Ted about what he's going to do after high school.

Ted: Are you in your last year of **high school**?

John: Yes, I'll be finished in a few months from now.

Ted: Congratulations! Did you **apply to university**?

John: Yes, for the University of Toronto. I get **good grades,** so I should get in. I even hope to **get a scholarship.**

Ted: That's great! Did you **choose a major**?

John: Not yet. Everyone does **general studies** in their **first year**. But next year, I want to choose something so I can have a **good salary** when I graduate.

Ted: Makes sense to me.

Vocabulary

high school: Last 3-4 years of school (approximately grades 9-12).

apply to university: Send in an application to go to university.

good grades: High marks in classes (mostly A's).

get a scholarship: Free money for university.

choose a major: Pick a course of study at university.

not yet: Not made a decision; haven't done something but plan to in the future.

general studies: Not specific classes.

first year: Year one of something, usually university.

good salary: Getting paid a lot of money to do a job.

makes sense: Has good logic.

Practice

1. That _____ to me why he would choose to change jobs.

2. I don't have to _____ until second year.

3. What _____ did you graduate from?

4. He didn't get _____ so has to retake some classes.

5. I'm planning on taking _____ in my first year.

6. The most important thing to me is a job with a _____.

7. I think I can _____ for university next year.

8. I'm in my _____. I just started last month.

9. My son is so lazy that I think he might not even _____.

10. Did you take out the trash? _____.

Answers

1. makes sense

2. choose a major

3. high school

4. good grades

5. general studies

6. good salary

7. get a scholarship

8. first year

9. apply to university

10. not yet

Cumbersome

Ali and Kiyo are talking about the lecture they both attended.

Ali: Kiyo, did you understand anything from that **lecture**? You have a **knack** for this stuff. It was all Greek to me. Like I don't think I understood anything. I feel like such an **amateur**.

Kiyo: You know the secret? I learned a lot of the **technical jargon** that **pertains** to it. That's what made a huge difference for me. Just **allocate** some time to it.

Ali: That's so smart. I think that would really help me too. It's so **cumbersome** to look up words that I don't know during lectures. Then I end up missing more stuff.

Kiyo: Exactly. That was my situation last semester. And hey, don't **hesitate** to ask me for help. I don't mind at all.

Ali: Sure. Thanks so much, my friend!

Vocabulary

lecture: A talk given to an audience, often at a college or university.

knack: A special skill or talent.

amateur: Not highly skilled in a particular area.

technical: Relating to a specific subject.

jargon: Words specific to a certain thing.

pertains: Relates to.

allocate: Put aside for a specific purpose.

cumbersome: Clumsy.

hesitate: To pause.

Vocabulary Challenge

1. Keith really has a _____ for playing soccer.

2. I'd like to _____ some time to clean the garage this weekend. What do you think?

3. That article is quite _____, but it's still worth a read.

4. One of my favorite artists is giving a _____ tomorrow night. Do you want to go with me?

5. I can help you fix your dishwasher, but to be honest, I'm pretty _____ at this kind of thing.

6. These directions are too _____. Can we make them simpler.

7. Hey, please don't _____ to reach out if you need some help moving.

8. What does all this _____ mean? It seems like a different language.

9. This meeting will _____ to what we're going to do with this advertising campaign. Let's not discuss other things like personnel.

Answers

1. knack

2. allocate

3. technical

4. lecture

5. amateur

6. cumbersome

7. hesitate

8. jargon

9. pertain

Break Through

Jerry is talking to Athena about her thesis.

Jerry: How's your thesis going?

Athena: I had a big **break through**. I'm planning to **hand it in** next month.

Jerry: Wow! That's great news. It was **hanging over** your head for so long. What did you **come up with**?

Athena: I'll **spare you** the boring details! But, I'm going to **make for** the mountains and **rip up** the slopes for a few days when it's done. That's the exciting news.

Jerry: I'll have to **see about sneaking in** a few days myself. I heard there was a big dump of snow last week.

Vocabulary

break through: Achieve some success at something, usually after a difficult period of time.

hand it in: Turn something in to a boss or teacher.

hanging over: Feeling upset or worried about something.

come up with: Discover; figure out.

spare you: Save from dealing with or hearing about.

make for: Go to.

rip up: Do a sport enthusiastically (skiing, snowboarding, skateboarding).

see about: Look into something.

sneaking in: Being able to do something even though you're busy; go someplace you're not supposed to go.

Vocabulary Challenge

1. I think someone is _____ here at night. Some things are in different spots each morning.

2. What did you _____?

3. I'll have to _____ that vacation request. I'm not sure what our staffing needs are yet.

4. I'm happy to _____ the hassle and just do it myself.

5. Please _____ by Friday at midnight.

6. Let's _____ the slopes this weekend! There's 100 cm of fresh snow!

7. He's famous for projects _____ his head for months until he finally gets them done.

8. Let's _____ the mountains! It's such a nice day.

9. We just had a big _____ on that research we're doing.

Answers

1. sneaking in

2. come up with

3. see about

4. spare you

5. hand it in

6. rip up

7. hanging over

8. make for

9. break through

Ph.D Options

Toby is talking to Ken about where he's going to do his Ph.D.

Ken: Have you decided where you want to do your **Ph.D.** yet?

Toby: I'm **sitting on the fence** for now! I haven't chosen a **specific** professor or university. But I want to be an **international student,** so I'm considering Europe.

Ken: Oh, how exciting! Which country?

Toby: I'm not sure yet. I'm applying for some **scholarships**. I don't want to live in **poverty**. It **boils down to** housing. I want a place that has **dormitory** options for **mature students**.

Ken: Well, I'm sure you'll **figure it out**. Any **university** would be lucky to have you.

Vocabulary

Ph.D.: Highest academic degree. Often necessary to become a professor at a university or college. A master's is a 1–2 year program that can prepare you for a career. A PhD, or doctoral degree, takes 3–7 years and prepares you for a career in academic research.

sitting on the fence: Not deciding about something.

specific: A certain thing, preference, etc.

international student: Someone who goes to school in another country.

scholarships: Free money that covers a part of or all tuition (and sometimes books/housing).

poverty: The state of being very poor.

boils down to: Refers to the most important thing or aspect of a situation.

dormitory: A place where students live, usually on campus.

mature students: Refers to a student who is older than other students in a year or program.

figure it out: Decide on something.

university: Usually an educational institute that offers 4 year undergraduate degrees, master's degree programs, and Ph.D. programs. Also known as "college" in some countries (for example, the USA).

Vocabulary Challenge

1. Only a few people are planning to do a _____ when we're done with this program.

2. I'm applying for lots of _____, but I haven't heard back yet.

3. Is there a _____ reason why I got a C on this paper? I'd like to improve for the next one.

4. Which _____ did you go to?

5. I'm _____ about which program to take. Both options seem good.

6. Most students live in conditions close to _____. They just don't have much money.

7. There are many _____ in my program.

8. I lived in the _____ my first two years of college.

9. Let me take a look at the numbers and see if I can _____.

10. I'm not sure which job I'll take but it will probably _____ salary.

11. An _____ at UBC has to pay $50,000 a year in tuition. It's so expensive!

Answers

1. Ph.D.

2. scholarships

3. specific

4. university

5. sitting on the fence

6. poverty

7. mature students

8. dormitory

9. figure it out

10. boil down to

11. international student

Bury my head in the sand

Meaning: To avoid a certain situation or problem.

Origin: Possibly related to ostriches who some observe to hide their heads in bushes when faced with predators. However, this isn't what they do!

Example TOEFL question: What can be done to alleviate poverty?

Possible answer: There's a lot that can be done but it's easier for politicians to *bury their heads in the sand* than to deal with it. . .

Call it a day

Meaning: To stop working for the rest of the day.

Origin: First recorded use was in 1919 to refer to the end of a workday.

Example TOEFL question: How can someone be a better employee?

Possible answer: One thing that most people could do, no matter the job, is to take a look around before they *call it a day* and make sure that they've tied up all the loose ends. I like to use the last 15 minutes of my day to make sure everything is ready for me to start work the following day.

Calm before the storm

Meaning: A quiet period before a difficult period.

Origin: Used by sailors to explain the eerily calm period before a big storm.

Example TOEFL question: What is the main environmental problem in your country?

Possible answer: The biggest problem not just in my country but in the world is global warming. We're in the *calm before the storm* right now, but I think we'll see the world get exponentially warmer in the coming years.

Can't put my finger on it

Meaning: Not sure exactly what is wrong.

Origin: From the 1800s. Refers to looking through a document and putting your finger onto something to support what you're looking for. If you can't find what you're looking for, then you can't put your finger on it.

Example TOEFL question: How do you distinguish fake news from real news?

Possible answer: I mean, you often *can't put your finger on it* but it's a feeling you get when you're reading or looking at something. If it's too outside the norm, then people should check it against other resources to see if it matches up.

Compare apples to oranges

Meaning: When people try to compare two things that shouldn't be compared because they're too different.

Origin: In use since the late 1800s. Predated by the idiom, "apples to oysters" in the 1600s as two things that could never be compared.

Example TOEFL question: What is the difference between white-collar jobs and blue-collar jobs?

Possible answer: These days, comparing blue-collar and white-collar jobs is like *comparing apples to oranges*. Machines are doing more of the physical labour and repetitive tasks and many of the traditionally blue-collar jobs require using computers.

Famine

Sam and Carrie are talking about a famine.

Sam: Have you heard about the **famine** in ABC country?

Carrie: I have. It seems really bad, but I don't know much about it. Is it an **anomaly** or an **annual** thing?

Sam: Oh, it happens every year. Experts **attribute** it to XYZ country **diverting** and taking a **disproportionate** amount of water from the main river running through both countries.

Carrie: So frustrating and sad. Water shouldn't be a **finite** resource. Of course this would **impoverish** that country if it were happening every single year. We need to **augment** our financial aid to poorer countries.

Vocabulary

famine: Extreme lack of food (usually at the country level).

anomaly: Something that is not the norm.

annual: Occurring yearly.

attribute: Give credit to.

diverting: Change of course.

disproportionate: Too large or too smart compared to something else.

finite: Having an end or limit.

impoverish: To reduce to poverty.

augment: Increase, or make larger.

Vocabulary Challenge

1. That _____ has killed hundreds of thousands of people so far.

2. Rich countries use a _____ amount of fossil fuels.

3. We won! It was kind of an _____. A small miracle.

4. The government didn't intend to _____ that whole group of people but that was the effect.

5. We have to stop _____ funds away from advertising. It's short-sighted.

6. Where are you going for your _____girl's trip?

7. We have _____ money. There has to be a way to reduce our budget each month.

8. You didn't come up with this idea on your own. You need to _____ it.

Answers

1. famine

2. disproportionate

3. anomaly

4. impoverish

5. diverting

6. annual

7. finite

8. attribute

Protecting the Environment

Jimmy and Kent are talking about the need to protect the environment.

Jimmy: So what are you doing your **final project** on?

Kent: The need to **protect the environment. Climate change** is real, **fossil fuels** are **running out,** and **natural disasters** are **on the rise**. It's scary stuff!

Jimmy: You're **preaching to the choir** here. I've been talking about **global warming** and the need to develop more sources of **renewable energy** for years.

Kent: Okay, good to hear! I've learned a lot from this project and want to tell everyone.

Vocabulary

final project: The last assignment to do for a class at school.

protect the environment: Do things to reduce harm to the Earth. For example, recycling or buying fewer things.

climate change: Changes in weather patterns, due to increasing temperatures on the Earth.

fossil fuels: Non-renewable energy sources like coal, oil, and gas.

running out: Being depleted.

natural disasters: Things like earthquakes, tornadoes, forest fires, etc.

on the rise: Increasing.

preaching to the choir: Telling someone something that they already know.

global warming: The Earth's average temperature increasing.

renewable energy: Energy source that doesn't run out. For example, solar or wind.

Vocabulary Challenge

1. We need to develop more _____ sources.

2. Our main goal is to _____. We think you'll find it easy to get on board with this.

3. Crime is _____ in my city.

4. _____ is a serious issue, probably the most important one facing our world today.

5. What are you going to do for your _____?

6. I'm hoping that cars won't run on _____ in 10 years from now.

7. There were so many _____ in 2020, probably due to climate change.

8. Honestly, you're _____ here. I already know this!

9. Time is _____ for us to decide what we're going to do.

Answers

1. renewable energy

2. protect the environment

3. on the rise

4. global warming/climate change

5. final project

6. fossil fuels

7. natural disasters

8. preaching to the choir

9. running out

Survey Design

Jen is talking with her professor about a survey that she's designing.

Professor: How's that **survey** design coming?

Jen: Well, I'm having kind of a difficult time with it. I know you mentioned that **bias** is a real thing and that we need to **compensate** for it in the design.

Professor: Yes, you have to, for sure. And also allow for a **margin of error** in the results because of this. If you send it over to me, I can have a look at what you have so far.

Jen: Sure, I'm almost done. I just have to **transfer** my rough notes into something you can understand! I also need some advice on how to reach my **target audience** and get parental **consent** since they're under 18, but that's a question for another day! I don't want to **violate** any kind of **ethical standards**.

Professor: Yes, and **put your thinking cap on**. I think you can **brainstorm** a bunch of ideas for that. But we can talk about that in our next meeting.

Vocabulary

survey: Questions that a researcher asks a group of people to find data.

bias: In favor of one thing or group of people over another.

compensate: Allow for something.

margin of error: Amount allowed for miscalculation.

transfer: Move something.

target audience: The people you intend to reach.

consent: Give permission; say "yes" to something.

violate: Break or not respect a rule or agreement.

ethical standards: Principles and morals that can guide decisions.

put your thinking cap on: Think deeply about something.

brainstorm: Come up with many ideas, quickly, without judging their validity.

Vocabulary Challenge

1. Please _____ at least 10 of your classmates.

2. You'll have to get the data from Ted. He can _____ it to a USB stick for you.

3. You'll need to get _____ from the parents if you want to talk to those kids.

4. Remember to _____ for the higher altitude in your calculations.

5. Be sure to talk to me first before doing anything. I don't want you to _____ any regulations with regards to testing on animals.

6. I hate working with ABC company. They have no _____.

7. Why don't we _____ a few ideas for our presentation topic?

8. Most people have a _____ towards attractive people.

9. My _____ is women, aged 20-29 who live in Canada.

10. Just _____. I know you'll come up with something.

11. What's the _____ in this survey?

Answers

1. survey

2. transfer

3. consent

4. compensate

5. violate

6. ethical standards

7. brainstorm

8. bias

9. target audience

10. put your thinking cap on

11. margin of error

An Ethical Issue

A TA is talking about an issue that he wants his students to discuss in an Ethics class.

Here's the situation that I want you to discuss in small groups. A large **manufacturer** of infant formula had two recipes. One of them, containing all the recommended vitamins and minerals, is for sale in countries like the USA, Canada, and Australia. The other one, which is cheaper to make, doesn't contain the **optimal** nutritional balance but instead has some **fillers** in it. It is an **inferior** product in almost all ways and is sold in countries with fewer governmental **regulations** about this kind of thing. It doesn't kill the babies, but they don't get **adequate** nutrition to **thrive**.

I want you to talk about who's to **blame**. Is it the government in those poorer countries for not having better regulations and **oversight**? Or, is the company negligent and should be **punished** for selling an inferior product? Or, are the parents somehow at fault? The parents are desperate for someone to answer for this, and the company narrowly avoided bankruptcy once the scandal became public knowledge.

Vocabulary

manufacturer: A company that makes things.

optimal: Ideal.

fillers: Something cheap that is added to something to make it less expensive to make.

inferior: Not as good.

regulations: Rules or laws about something.

adequate: Acceptable; good enough.

thrive: Do well.

blame: Responsibility for something that went wrong.

oversight: Inspections for quality control purposes.

punished: Consequences for doing something against the law or unethical practices.

Vocabulary Challenge

1. There are only a few _____ left in my town.

2. His meals don't have _____ nutrition in them. I'm worried he'll get sick.

3. That company should get _____ for selling such a terrible product.

4. He seems to _____ with a heavier workload. It's impressive.

5. It's cheaper, but it's an _____ product. You won't be happy with it.

6. This hamburger doesn't taste good. I think it has lots of _____ in it.

7. Who's to _____ here? Tom and Jerry were working on that project together.

8. The government should have more _____ about medical testing on humans.

9. It sounds like that department needs some more _____. They keep making mistakes.

10. The _____ balance for most meals is equal parts fat, carbs, and protein.

Answers

1. manufacturers

2. adequate

3. punished

4. thrive

5. inferior

6. fillers

7. blame

8. regulations

9. oversight

10. optimal

Fundamental Flaws

Lindsey and Sam are talking about an assignment.

Lindsey: So what do we have to do? I didn't understand. **Compare** and **contrast** Sweden and Canada's responses to Covid-19?

Sam: Yes, exactly. We have to give a **summary** of the **response** of each country, along with a **timeline**. Essentially, **trace** the spread of the virus. Then comment on any **fundamental flaws** or **errors** that they made trying to reduce the number of deaths.

Lindsey: Okay, I see. So I guess the **desired outcome** is the same for each country—to **minimize** the number of deaths. They just went about it differently.

Sam: Yes, I've started doing some research. It's quite interesting to see the differing actions and resulting **statistics**.

Vocabulary

compare: Look for the similarities in two or more things.

contrast: Look for the differences in two or more things.

summary: Brief overview.

response: Action taken as a result of something that happened.

timeline: Arranging events by time from the beginning to end.

trace: Find or uncover a source or course of something after some investigation.

fundamental flaws: Underlying problems in the basic design or substance of a thing.

errors: Mistakes

desired outcome: Best possible result.

minimize: Make smaller or lesser.

Vocabulary Challenge

1. Please _____ the findings from these two papers.

2. There are so many _____ with this project. Nothing we do now can fix it.

3. Please try to _____ your mistakes in the lab or you won't get accurate results.

4. I didn't read the entire thing—just the _____.

5. Can you _____ Covid-19 infections using social media posts?

6. The _____ between rainfall in Vancouver and Riyadh is striking.

7. The _____ is that everyone will pass this class but that's mostly up to you.

8. What's the _____ here? I need to understand who did what first.

9. Why is this returning so many _____? We've done something wrong.

10. Trudeau's _____ to Covid-19 was okay but not what I would have done.

Answers

1. compare

2. fundamental flaws

3. minimize

4. summary

5. trace

6. contrast

7. desired outcome

8. timeline

9. errors

10. response

Lifestyle Changes

Kim is talking to Tanya about her health.

Kim: Did you **go to the doctor**? I know you were **not feeling well**.

Tanya: I did. She didn't **diagnose me** with anything but said that I'd need to make some serious **lifestyle changes**. My **overall health** is quite poor.

Kim: Oh no! What did she recommend?

Tanya: She said that I have to **reduce my stress**, **get plenty of sleep**, and **eat a balanced diet**.

Kim: That doesn't sound so bad. Do you have to **quit smoking**?

Tanya: Oh yeah, that too. It **shook me up**. She said that if I didn't change, my **life expectancy** would decrease.

Vocabulary

go to the doctor: Have an appointment with a doctor.

not feeling well: Feeling sick.

diagnose me: Assign a name to a health problem.

lifestyle changes: Change in what you eat, how much you exercise and other unhealthy habits like smoking or drinking alcohol.

overall health: General level of healthiness/unhealthiness.

reduce my stress: Decrease the amount of stress in your life.

get plenty of sleep: Sleep eight hours a night.

eat a balanced diet: Eating mostly healthy food from all the food groups.

quit smoking: Stop using cigarettes.

shook me up: Made me feel nervous, worried, or anxious.

life expectancy: How long you can expect to live.

Practice

1. In Canada, the average _____ for men is 84 years.

2. Please _____. It seems like you've been sick for a while now.

3. You'll have to make some _____ to reduce your chance of a heart attack.

4. It _____ when he told me that he wanted to get divorced.

5. I'm _____. I need to go home early today.

6. I hope that I can _____ by changing jobs.

7. My goal is to _____ this year but I know it won't be easy.

8. Please try to _____ if you want to lower your cholesterol.

9. My doctor didn't _____ with anything but just said that I had to stop drinking so much coffee.

10. His _____ is quite good, considering how old he is.

11. Please try to _____ before your exam. You'll be able to think more clearly.

Answers

1. life expectancy

2. go to the doctor

3. lifestyle changes

4. shook me up

5. not feeling well

6. reduce my stress

7. quit smoking

8. eat a balanced diet

9. diagnose me

10. overall health

11. get plenty of sleep

Confusing Words: Bored/Boring

bored: An adjective that describes when someone is uninterested in what is happening. The feeling someone experiences.

I'm so bored. This movie is terrible.

If you're bored, go play outside.

I feel bored when I'm hanging out alone.

boring: An adjective that describes the person, thing, or object that is causing the uninterested feeling. The cause of the feeling.

Don't you think this movie is boring?

My teacher is so boring. Most of the students are sleeping.

I find watching golf on TV really boring.

Tip for other ed/ing adjectives: You can use this general rule for adjectives that end in ed/ing.

adjective + —ed = A feeling. Examples: tired, disinterested, confused, scared.

adjective + —ing = Cause of feeling. Examples: tiring, uninteresting, confusing.

I'm tired because studying math is tiring.

I'm confused. My teacher's directions for the homework are confusing.

Horror movies are terrifying. I feel so scared when I watch them.

Vocabulary Challenge

1. I'm _____ because my class is _____.

2. When do you feel _____?

3. Everyone loves watching "Friends," but I think it's _____.

4. Do you really want to watch "Frozen" again? Isn't it _____ after so many times?

5. Ugghhh . . . spaghetti again? I'm so _____ of that.

6. Reading the newspaper is _____. I'd rather watch the news on TV.

Answers

1. bored, boring

2. bored

3. boring

4. boring

5. bored

6. boring

Extra practice. Fill in the blanks with different _ed, _ing words:

1. I feel _____ when I _____.

2. My friend feels _____ when he/she _____.

3. I feel _____ when I _____.

4. My boss feels _____ when he/she _____.

Hold On

Mickey and Tanya are trying to solve a problem.

Mickey: So I think we can **head back** to work now. Let's just **keep to** our original plan.

Tanya: **Hold on** a second. Sorry to **butt in** like this but I think we need to **back up** a bit here. This problem isn't going to **go away** if we do nothing about it. We need to change something up.

Mickey: So what do you suggest?

Tanya: I think we need to **come back** to the original question and see if there's a more creative way of looking for solutions. There must be. Then we need to choose one of them and **stick with** the plan across the board.

Mickey: Okay, you're right. Back to the drawing board. Let's get this problem solved!

Tanya: And for **subsequent** problems, I don't want us to stick our heads in the sand.

Vocabulary

head back: Go back to something.

keep to: Stick with something.

hold on: Wait.

butt in: Interrupt.

back up: Return to a previous thing.

go away: Leave.

come back: Return.

stick with: Not give up.

subsequent: Coming after something.

Vocabulary Challenge

1. I'm going to _____ home now. I'm so tired.

2. Let's make dinner when you _____ from your run.

3. Sorry to _____ like this but I think it's an emergency.

4. Let's _____ and start at the beginning. I think I lost you somewhere there.

5. Let's try to _____ the schedule, okay?

6. His work had a big impact on _____ scholars.

7. Can you _____? I don't want to talk to you right now. I'm still angry.

8. I know it's difficult to learn to play guitar but _____ it.

9. Please _____ a second. I'll help you when I'm done with this customer.

Answers

1. head back

2. come back

3. butt in

4. back up

5. keep to

6. subsequent

7. go away

8. stick with

9. hold on

The Environment

Sid and Drew are environmental science students who are discussing an issue.

Sid: Hey Drew. Did you hear that **greenhouse gas emissions** have gone way down since Covid started?

Drew: Oh yeah. I heard that. That's good news, but I'm not sure it's enough to combat **rising sea levels** and the **melting ice caps** due to decades of overconsumption and pollution. Not to mention all the holes in the **ozone layer**. **In the long run**, it won't make much difference.

Sid: Oh, I hear you. We need to develop more **clean energy** sources. The old **reduce, reuse and recycle** thing isn't good enough. We need **systemic change**.

Drew: I **totally agree** with you. Global warming will lead to humanity's **ultimate** demise.

Vocabulary

greenhouse gas emissions: What is released (mainly carbon dioxide) when fossil fuels are burned.

rising sea levels: How the level of the ocean is increasing year after year.

melting ice caps: There is less ice at the North and South poles because they are melting due to climate change.

in the long run: Over a long period of time.

ozone layer: A layer in the atmosphere that absorbs the UV rays from the sun.

clean energy: Renewable energy like wind, water, and sun.

reduce, reuse, recycle: A slogan about what people can do to help the environment.

systemic change: Change that happens from the top, usually at the government level.

totally agree: Complete agreement about something.

ultimate: The last or final thing.

Vocabulary Challenge

1. We need to do more as a country to reduce _____.

2. We can each do our part to save the environment, but _____ is also important.

3. Some people will have to leave their island homes in the next few years because of _____.

4. We can all do more to _____.

5. I _____ with you about this! You don't have to convince me.

6. The holes in the _____ are getting bigger and bigger each year.

7. The _____ downfall of our world will be water scarcity.

8. Polar bears are having a difficult time because of the _____.

9. Changing to an electric car will save money _____.

10. Wind and solar power are examples of _____.

Answers

1. greenhouse gas emissions

2. systemic change

3. rising sea levels

4. reduce, reuse, and recycle

5. totally agree

6. ozone layer

7. ultimate

8. melting ice caps

9. in the long run

10. clean energy

At Risk

Tom is talking to Jennifer about his sketchy coworker.

Jennifer: So, what's new at work?

Tom: Oh, I forgot to tell you. That guy Bob that I've mentioned before put our whole company **at risk**. Profits were **in decline**, but nobody could figure out why. It turns out our main competitor was paying him to sabotage the production line.

Jennifer: Oh wow. How did you figure it out?

Tom: Only **by luck**. We **speculated** he was the problem, but had no proof. We installed security cameras, but Bob didn't know about it. He got caught destroying a key piece of machinery.

Jennifer: Wow. He didn't act **in good faith**. But I guess there was no way to know that he'd go rogue at the outset.

Tom: Anyone can turn bad for enough money, I guess. It might be hard to **resist**.

Vocabulary

at risk: Exposed to harm.

in decline: Going down (often refers to health or financial things).

by luck: Success or failure caused by chance.

speculated: Formed a theory without evidence.

in good faith: With good intentions.

resist: Withstand.

Vocabulary Challenge

1. That whole industry is _____. I wonder what happened?

2. I don't think things happen _____. All you need is hard work.

3. You can _____ anything if you put your mind to it.

4. That other company didn't negotiate _____.

5. We _____ for years about Bob and Cara, but they would never admit they were dating.

6. My business is _____ because I just lost a key employee.

Answers

1. in decline

2. by luck

3. resist

4. in good faith

5. speculated

6. at risk

Corner the market

Meaning: Gain a lot of the market share.

Origin: Unknown, but likely originated in the 1800s with the beginning of the market economy.

Example TOEFL question: Describe a company whose products you love.

Possible answer: It's maybe a bit of a cliche, but I love Apple products. They have *cornered the market* in the personal computer and smartphone space because their products are so intuitive and also very high in quality. I find that they're far more durable than something from Dell or Toshiba, for example.

Crunch the numbers

Meaning: Analyze data.

Origin: Came into use in the 1980s when computers became more commonplace and refers to the complicated numerical calculations that mainframe computers did at the time.

Example TOEFL question: Describe something that you bought recently.

Possible answer: I bought a big thing recently—a condo! I wasn't sure I could afford it here in Vancouver, but a mortgage broker *crunched the numbers* and made it work. I'm going to be moving in next month.

Fall through the cracks

Meaning: Overlook something.

Origin: Unknown. However, it's easy to imagine small cracks in old wooden floors and things going missing.

Example TOEFL question: What can be done to alleviate poverty?

Possible answer: Poor people often *fall through the cracks* when it comes to things like medical and dental services. The government should provide free clinics for people who are unable to access these things.

Feeling the pinch

Meaning: Experiencing financial difficulties.

Origin: From the 1800s. Could be related to having to tighten a belt when there is less food to eat. Or, kids who have to wear shoes that are too small and getting their toes pinched because parents couldn't afford to buy new ones.

Example TOEFL question: What social problems are there in your country?

Possible answer: The USA, like most countries, is *feeling the pinch* from Covid-19 and there's less money to go around for things like homeless or unemployed people. These problems are only going to get worse as time goes on.

Get into deep water

Meaning: To be in trouble.

Origin: From Psalm 69:14 in the Bible, "...out of the deep waters."

Example TOEFL question: Do you think that most companies are ethical?

Possible answer: There are some good companies out there but if you look at the news, there are always stories of businesses *getting into deep water* for one reason or the other.

Key Role

Sally and Marty are talking about hiring somebody.

Sally: Hey Marty, we need to talk about Tom leaving. It's a **key role** we have to fill thoughtfully. We have a **tendency to** rush through the **hiring process,** but it's such a **demanding job** that I don't think we can do that this time.

Marty: Of course, I agree 100% with you. I'm interested in that guy Jim Jones. Do you remember him? He **did a presentation** at that conference we were at.

Sally: I was **impressed with** him too. He won't just **quit his job** though! We'll have to pay him an extremely **competitive salary** to get him to leave.

Marty: I'll **ask around,** and see people in that position are getting paid **these days**.

Vocabulary

key role: An important position.

tendency to: Usually acts in a certain way.

hiring process: Putting up a job ad, taking applications, doing interviews, etc. From start to finish.

demanding job: A job that is difficult and time-consuming.

did a presentation: Spoke in front of other people about a certain topic.

impressed with: Felt admiration or respect for.

quit his job: Gave notice that he would stop working at his job.

competitive salary: A salary that is similar to what other companies are paying.

ask around: Enquire.

these days: Recently; now.

Vocabulary Challenge

1. _____, I've been working a lot. Nothing too exciting.

2. Let me _____. I'm sure someone knows a good plumber.

3. Let's fast-track the _____. We needed someone yesterday.

4. The CFO is a _____ in all organizations.

5. I _____ at the conference last year, but I think I'm going to skip this year.

6. A _____ for a good salesperson is more than $100,000.

7. He has a _____ to rush through his homework, so he can play video games.

8. I think he should _____. What a terrible boss.

9. It's a _____, but it also comes with a very high salary.

10. I'm _____ how well he did on that test.

Answers

1. these days

2. ask around

3. hiring process

4. key role

5. did a presentation

6. competitive salary

7. tendency to

8. quit his job

9. demanding job

10. impressed with

For the Long Haul

A professor is talking about ABC Car Company in an Economics class.

Professor: ABC Car Company is considering **scaling back** production on Model 1234. It's their largest SUV and is known for being a serious **gas guzzler**. This is due to **skyrocketing** fuel prices and also the fact that there isn't as much demand these days for vehicles that aren't **fuel-efficient**. They're going to put it on the **backburner** for now.

Student: *Is this the plan **for the long haul**? Or just until gas prices go back down to normal levels?*

Professor: They'll stick with their current plan, I think. **Pretty much** as long as fuel prices remain at current levels and they're **in the red**, they won't make a change. They're **feeling the pinch** with their expansion into Canada and Europe and don't have **money to burn** like they did a few years ago. They can't afford to bleed money on this model like they might have been willing to do in the past.

Vocabulary

scaling back: Reducing how much/many of a product will be made.

gas guzzler: A vehicle that uses a lot more gas than an average car.

skyrocketing: Increasing rapidly.

fuel-efficient: Doesn't use much energy, compared to similar products.

backburner: Leave something for now and deal with it later.

for the long haul: For the long term.

pretty much: Almost 100% certain.

in the red: Losing money.

feeling the pinch: Experiencing financial difficulties.

money to burn: Extra money to spend freely.

Vocabulary Challenge

1. Look at that new car he bought. He must have _____.

2. My company is in it _____.

3. The most important feature for a new car is that it has to be _____ because of my long commute.

4. I'm worried about this project that's now running _____.

5. We're _____ with Covid-19. There are so many extra costs to doing business now.

6. I _____ will never buy anything from that company again. They have terrible customer service.

7. Let's put this on the _____ until the economy recovers.

8. Fuel prices are _____ these days with the shortages.

9. That enormous SUV looks nice but isn't it a _____? It'll be so expensive to use.

10. Let's think about _____ production until the new model comes out.

Answers

1. money to burn

2. for the long haul

3. fuel-efficient

4. in the red

5. feeling the pinch

6. pretty much

7. backburner

8. skyrocketing

9. gas guzzler

10. scaling back

Confusing Words: e.g. / i.e.

Even many native English speakers don't know the difference between these two abbreviations. Both are used mainly in writing.

e.g.: Same as "for example." Used before an item or list of items that serve as examples for the previous statement.

The abbreviation "e.g." stands for the Latin phrase *exempli gratia*, meaning "for example."

Tip: Say this as "E (pause) G."

Please don't come to the ER for minor things, e.g. small cuts, headaches, or minor burns.

I prefer to live in a sustainable city (e.g. with a high walkability score, electric car charging stations, and farmer's markets).

I'm trying to eat healthier (e.g. more veggies and fewer fatty snacks).

i.e.: Used to restate something previously said to clarify meaning.

The abbreviation "i.e." stands for *id est*, which is Latin for "that is."

Tip: Say this as "I (pause) E."

The table shows that all populations in all states but one increased because of natural causes (i.e. more births than deaths).

If your home has hard water (i.e. a high mineral content), then you may notice a yellow film in your sink and bathtub.

We're hoping to have most people (i.e. at least 90%) vaccinated by the end of the year.

Vocabulary Challenge

1. Make sure you pack well for the hike (_____ first aid kit, extra socks, water, snacks, and rain gear).

2. The fifth amendment (_____ what allows people to not answer questions that might incriminate them) is how he got around answering the questions.

3. You can't cover up basic flaws (_____ a cracked foundation or leaking roof) with a coat of paint.

4. Only 10-12 year olds can register (_____ between Jan. 1st, 2010 and Dec. 31St, 2012).

5. After work, let's meet at the new restaurant, _____ Luigi's.

6. My city has so many problems (_____ high crime rate, terrible schools, and lack of jobs) that I'm thinking of moving.

Answers

1. e.g.

2. i.e.

3. e.g.

4. i.e.

5. i.e.

6. e.g.

Indefatigable

Emma and Ash are college students who are talking about their summer plans.

Emma: So what are your summer plans? I'm sure you have some **ambitious** plans in the works?

Ash: I'll be interning at ABC financial as a junior analyst.

Emma: Of course you are! You have the right **attitude** for that—**continuously** looking to learn more. You're so **dynamic** and **indefatigable** too.

Ash: What's your plan?

Emma: Well, I'm happy with something **mediocre** and **stable**! I'll probably work at my uncle's manufacturing company.

Ash: That sounds fine. May we both **prosper** and be happy this summer doing our things!

Emma: Yes, I hope so.

Vocabulary

ambitious: Having large goals.

attitude: Manner or feeling.

continuously: Going without stopping.

dynamic: Constantly changing.

indefatigable: Without tiring.

mediocre: Average or ordinary.

stable: Unlikely to change or fail.

prosper: To do well.

Vocabulary Challenge

1. He's an _____ guy who will go far in life.

2. I wish I had _____ amounts of energy like you do.

3. With the right _____, you can accomplish almost anything.

4. I played professional hockey, but I was a very _____ player.

5. I hope that you _____ during 2023.

6. My goal is to _____ improve at tennis.

7. I just want to get a _____ job when I graduate. I don't even care how much they pay me.

8. Why don't we talk to Sharon Carr. She's a _____ speaker and would be perfect for our retreat.

Answers

1. ambitious

2. indefatigable

3. attitude

4. mediocre

5. prosper

6. continuously

7. stable

8. dynamic

Knowledge-Based Economy

A TA is discussing an issue in an Economics tutorial.

Canada is now a **knowledge-based economy**. Workers who ignore that do so at their own **peril**. Most of the **manufacturing** jobs, and especially the good **union** jobs, have now been **outsourced** to places with cheaper labour like India or China. Those who lack the skills to operate in a digital world risk being left out of the **job market** altogether.

One option is **retraining**. However, that can be quite difficult with older workers who are not that familiar with using computers. It can be an **uphill battle**. However, there are some **alternatives** for these workers who get **laid off** from manufacturing jobs. Has anyone seen any approaches mentioned in the news lately? Let's talk about some of the new programs.

Vocabulary

knowledge-based economy: A kind of economy where information or intellectual skills are most important.

peril: Risk.

manufacturing: Making something.

union: An organization that negotiates for and protects a group of workers from employers.

outsourced: Work that is sent to another country, company, etc.

job market: Where employees look for jobs and employers look for workers.

retraining: Learning new skills for a different kind of job than currently doing.

uphill battle: Describes something very difficult to do or achieve.

alternatives: Other options.

laid off: A worker is temporarily or permanently stopped from working because of a situation out of their control.

Vocabulary Challenge

1. Older people often have a difficult time adapting to a _____.

2. The _____ is great for employees these days. Wages keep going up.

3. Good _____ jobs with benefits are difficult to find in Europe these days.

4. Learning computer skills later in life is an _____ for some people.

5. My company _____ customer service to India last year.

6. We'll have to switch to digital records soon. If we don't, it's at our own _____.

7. My wife got _____ when her company went out of business.

8. I might do some _____ and learn how to become a car mechanic.

9. Why don't you consider the _____ before making a decision? You're overlooking some of them.

10. The _____ dues (fees) are quite high but it's maybe worth it? The union did negotiate a good contract for us last year.

Answers

1. knowledge-based economy

2. job market

3. manufacturing

4. uphill battle

5. outsourced

6. peril

7. laid off

8. retraining

9. alternatives

10. union

In the Black

Ben is talking to Henry about his business.

Henry: How's business going these days, Ben? Are you **in the red** since Covid hit?

Ben: We were at first, but we're back **in the black** now. **Doing business** hasn't been easy these past few months.

Henry: You do so well, **pouring over the numbers** and making it work. I'm **all thumbs** with that kind of stuff.

Ben: You sure do know how to **pay someone a compliment**. Honestly, my secret is getting stuff done **well in advance**. I'd **go crazy** trying to do it all **last minute**.

Vocabulary

in the red: Losing money.

in the black: Making money.

doing business: Running a company.

pouring over the numbers: Looking closely at income, expenses, etc. for a home or business.

all thumbs: Not coordinated; clumsy.

pay someone a compliment: Say something kind about someone else. For example, "You look nice today."

well in advance: A long time before something needs to be done.

go crazy: Be stressed out.

last minute: Doing something at the last final possible moment.

Vocabulary Challenge

1. My company is _____ this quarter but we're hoping for better results later this year.

2. Why are we always finishing this stuff at the _____?

3. If you get your homework done _____, then you won't have as much stress in your life.

4. Having no free time is the cost of _____ in this industry.

5. Let's get back _____, okay? We'll have to push hard for it though.

6. I'd _____ if I had to commute to work every day.

7. I'm _____ when it comes to computer stuff.

8. I try to _____ every day.

9. I've been _____, and I just don't think we can afford to move.

Answers

1. in the red

2. last minute

3. well in advance

4. doing business

5. in the black

6. go crazy

7. all thumbs

8. pay someone a compliment

9. pouring over the numbers

Evolution

Lana and Cindy are talking about an article they read about the American education system.

Lana: You wouldn't believe what I read the other day. It was about the **debate** in the USA over what to teach in science classes—**evolution** or **creationism**.

Cindy: I've heard a bit about that. Most other countries **take it for granted** that the **theory** of evolution is a real thing. Not in the USA though. There are many people who **deny** it.

Lana: I know, there's so much evidence for it though. For example, **the fossil record**. Who could deny it? It's not controversial at all!

Cindy: Well, **the driving force** behind it is the Christian Church. They have a lot of **influence** over many spheres of life in the USA, including things like abortion rights.

Lana: I'm not sure why **Joe Public** has so much influence. Scientists should decide what to teach in science class.

Vocabulary

debate: Discussion where people have different viewpoints.

evolution: The theory that humans evolved from earlier forms like apes.

creationism: The theory that God created humans exactly as they are.

take it for granted: Assume that something is true, without questioning it.

theory: A system of ideas to explain something that may, or may not, be true.

deny: Say that something isn't true.

the fossil record: A scientific term. Refers to fossils and the information discovered through them.

the driving force: The power behind something.

influence: Affect someone or something.

Joe Public: The general public's attitude toward a topic (made into a single person).

Vocabulary Challenge

1. We can _____ about it all day, but I'm not going to change my mind.

2. You can't _____ that his presentation was excellent, even though you don't like him.

3. Abortion rights. You can't _____ in the USA.

4. How can you not believe in _____? It's clear we descended from apes.

5. You have more _____ with Tony than you think. He always listens to you.

6. In my opinion, evolution isn't a _____. There's so much evidence.

7. I don't care what _____ has to say about it. We need to do the right thing here.

8. The Catholic Church is _____ for many conservative viewpoints in the USA.

9. _____ shows that humans have evolved over millions of years.

10. Many religious people believe in _____.

Answers

1. debate

2. deny

3. take it for granted

4. evolution

5. influence

6. theory

7. Joe Public

8. the driving force

9. the fossil record

10. creationism

Housing in Vancouver

Kerry and Joe are talking about how expensive housing is after their Sociology class.

Kerry: Did you hear that the city of Vancouver is **taking action** to address **housing prices**?

Joe: What are they doing? I'd love to move, but **affordable housing** is hard to come by.

Kerry: I'm **in the same boat**. The city of Vancouver is building a new **housing development** and offering **low-interest rate** mortgages.

Joe: It's about time. Unless you **inherit money**, it's almost impossible for the **working Joe** to buy a house here.

Kerry: Well, **check into it,** and if you buy a place, invite me to your **housewarming party**!

Vocabulary

taking action: Doing something.

housing prices: The average price of houses in an area.

affordable housing: Housing that is designed to be cheaper than normal, usually subsidized by the government.

in the same boat: To be in the same bad situation.

housing development: An area in which the houses have all been planned and built at the same time in an organized way.

low-interest rates: When interest rates are lower than normal.

it's about time: Finally.

inherit money: Receiving money that someone left you in their will.

working Joe: The average working person.

check into it: Find out more information about something.

housewarming party: A party to celebrate moving into a new home.

Vocabulary Challenge

1. What are the average _____ in Victoria like?

2. Are you going to _____ when your parents die?

3. I'd love to get into that new _____ in the west end of the city.

4. I'm happy that the city is finally _____ on that guy across the street.

5. It's difficult for working families to buy a house in a place with no _____.

6. Congratulations on your new place! When's the _____?

7. Stop complaining. We're all _____.

8. Did he finally do his chores? _____.

9. I'm just an average _____, doing the 9-5.

10. I'm not sure about that. I'll have to _____.

11. It's a great time to buy a house when there are _____.

Answers

1. housing prices

2. inherit money

3. housing development

4. taking action

5. affordable housing

6. housewarming party

7. in the same boat

8. it's about time

9. working Joe

10. check into it

11. low-interest rates

Pull It Off

Ethan is talking to his friend about how stressed out he is.

Ethan: I'm feeling stressed out. I think I **bit off more than I can chew**.

Jeremiah: Yeah? What's up? Whatever it is, I'm sure that you can **pull it off.**

Ethan: Well, I had to **brush up on** a new programming language for a project I'm doing in one of my classes, but I'm not **catching on** as quickly as I usually do. The homework is starting to **pile up.** It's pure **drudgery**.

Jeremiah: Don't **freak out.** You're a smart guy! **Get on it,** and you'll be **up to speed** in no time. Soon, you'll be **showing off** like usual. Haha!

Ethan: Not likely, but thanks for your support. I want to **leave this behind** me as soon as possible!

Vocabulary

bit off more than I can chew: Choosing to do something that requires a lot more time and energy to do than you thought before starting the task.

pull it off: Succeed at doing something, usually difficult.

brush up on: Refresh; relearn something.

catching on: Understanding or figuring something out.

pile up: Not taking enough action so that projects or tasks increase to a stressful amount.

drudgery: Describes boring work.

freak out: Panic or feel extreme anxiety about something.

get on it: Start doing something.

up to speed: Describes someone who is fully informed or who has full knowledge.

showing off: Boasting or bragging.

leave this behind: Forget about it; finish it so I can forget about the stress.

Vocabulary Challenge

1. Stop _____! I already know that you're good at that.

2. If anyone can _____, it's you.

3. Tommy is famous for letting assignments _____ and then pulling all-nighters.

4. I think she's _____ quickly. I'm so happy with her progress.

5. Can we please _____ us? We keep coming back to it, but it's not helpful.

6. You'll get _____ here in a few months.

7. Math is pure _____ to me. I can't understand how some people find it interesting.

8. Okay, let's _____. We have so much to do.

9. Don't _____ about what I'm going to tell you, okay?

10. I need to _____ my high school math for this accounting class I'm taking.

11. I may have _____. I think I need some help with this big project if it's going to get done in time.

Answers

1. showing off

2. pull it off

3. pile up

4. catching on

5. leave this behind

6. up to speed

7. drudgery

8. get on it

9. freak out

10. brush up on

11. bit off more than I can chew

Confusing Words: For/Since

These prepositions of time can be a bit confusing because they both can be used for an event that began in the past and extends until now. However, there is a big difference to be aware of. Keep on reading to find out!

for: Used to refer to a period of time (for 10 years, for the whole summer).

I've played soccer for 10 years.

We've had our dog Rex for 3 years now.

It's been raining for days.

I'm going to try not smoking for a week and see how I feel.

since: Used to refer to a specific point in time when the activity began (since 2012, since I started high school). Note: "since I started high school" doesn't give the specific year, but it does imply a specific start date.

I've played soccer since I was 10 years old.

We've had our dog Rex since 2019.

It's been raining since 10:00 this morning.

I haven't had a drink of alcohol since last October.

Vocabulary Challenge

1. We've been in business _____ 1955.

2. You've already been here _____ hours. Let's go home.

3. I've wanted to do the Appalachian Trail _____ I read a book about it.

4. My son has played tennis _____ he was very young.

5. My children have been playing all kinds of sports _____ years.

6. I want to avoid meat _____ as long as possible. My doctor said that my cholesterol was so high.

Answers

1. since

2. for

3. since

4. since

5. for

6. for

Extra Practice: Write a sentence using "for." Make a sentence with the same meaning using "since." Do this 3 times.

For example:

I've loved pizza since I was a kid = I've loved pizza for 30 years.

Private Industry

A professor is talking about monopolies in an Economics class.

These days, there aren't that many true monopolies except in government-owned companies like the post office, as well as water, gas, and electric companies. One of the best examples of a **monopoly** in **private industry** is Google which has **the upper hand** in the world of search. There are other **legitimate** competitors like Yahoo and Microsoft, but they lag far behind in terms of market share and revenue.

Some people argue for government regulation of Google, but others think that they shouldn't interfere. After all, Google provides a **superior** product, and **consumers** are ultimately choosing to use them instead of someone else that also provides search results. Google has **state-of-the-art** servers and algorithms and seems to understand what people are looking for better than anyone else. **On the other hand**, companies like Yahoo maybe don't have an **incentive** to improve their results because the gap between the two is **insurmountable**.

Vocabulary

monopoly: Only one company that offers a specific product or service.

private industry: A company that isn't run by the government.

the upper hand: Having power or control in a situation. Having an advantage.

legitimate: In this situation, refers to real or competitive.

superior: Better.

consumers: People who buy things or use services.

state-of-the-art: The best of something, usually related to technology.

on the other hand: To compare and contrast one idea or thing versus another.

incentive: Something that motivates or encourages someone to do something.

insurmountable: Can't be overcome.

Vocabulary Challenge

1. The Smartphone industry is the opposite of a _____. There are many competitors.

2. Go in for the kill. You have _____.

3. I don't think healthcare should be delivered through _____.

4. There's no _____ to do well on the midterm exam. It's a pass-fail class.

5. You have a _____ concern, but I think we can handle it.

6. The university just built an expensive, _____ research lab.

7. The US economy depends on _____ buying things.

8. Kate just got a C on her essay. _____, she did do well on that last project.

9. Learning a new language is not _____. The key is getting started.

10. Go with the pro model. It's more expensive, but it's a _____ product.

Answers

1. monopoly

2. the upper hand

3. private industry

4. incentive

5. legitimate

6. state-of-the-art

7. consumers

8. on the other hand

9. insurmountable

10. superior

Give them a run for their money

Meaning: Provide good competition.

Origin: Could be from horse racing and placing bets. Sometimes horses are withdrawn from a race after bets are placed in which case you don't get a run for your money.

Example TOEFL question: Is there a certain brand of technology that you like using?

Possible answer: Sure, like most people, I love my iPhone. However, Samsung is starting to *give them a run for their money* these days, so I may switch to them for my next one.

Go the extra mile

Meaning: Work very hard to do a good job. Doing something extra than is expected.

Origin: From Matthew 5:41 in the Bible. Under Roman law, a soldier could order a Jew to carry his pack for a mile. Matthew said to carry it even further than that without complaint.

Example TOEFL question: What are some qualities of a good employee or student?

Possible answer: The best quality of a good employee or student is someone that will *go the extra mile* to get the task done. This applies to any job, industry, or educational setting. If someone doesn't care about results, they will only do the bare minimum.

Hit the books

Meaning: Study.

Origin: Unknown.

Example TOEFL question: What do you usually do in the evenings?

Possible answer: I know it's kind of boring, but in the evenings, I usually *hit the books.* I'm trying to become a chartered accountant and am doing classes at night.

In the driver's seat

Meaning: In control of something; able to make decisions.

Origin: First seen in the 1600s with "In the saddle." "In the driver's seat" came into common usage in the 1800s when cars became more popular.

Example TOEFL question: Describe a time when you had to make a difficult decision.

Possible answer: After university, I was fortunate enough to have three job offers. I was *in the driver's seat,* but it wasn't easy to choose between them. In the end, I went with the company offering the highest salary which I think was the correct decision.

In the same boat

Meaning: In a similar situation as someone else; or a situation where peoples' fates are tied together.

Origin: Various theories but one is that it was used by the ancient Greeks to refer to all the people in a boat facing the same fate when going out to sea. They would all either survive and make it, or sink and drown.

Example TOEFL question: Are most people addicted to social media?

Possible answer: Oh, we're all *in the same boat*—totally addicted! I watched a documentary about how companies like Facebook or Instagram design their platforms to be addictive.

Graduate from College

Liz is talking to Harry about her son.

Harry: How's Ethan doing at college?

Liz: Oh, no great. He's **failing a class** and didn't **pass a test** in another one. I'm not sure he even **takes notes** in his classes. I'm worried that he's never going to **graduate from college** or **get a degree**.

Harry: Didn't he **get good grades** in **middle school** and **high school**?

Liz: He did. That's the weird thing. We're trying to help him **get back on track**.

Harry: Hopefully it all **works out in the end**.

Vocabulary

failing a class: Not passing a course.

pass a test: Get over 50% on an exam.

takes notes: Attend a lecture (or meeting) and write down the main points.

graduate from college: Finish four years of university.

get a degree: Finish college and get the paper certificate proving that you did.

get good grades: Achieve higher than average grades in school.

middle school: Approximately grades 7-9.

high school: Approximately grades 10-12.

get back on track: Start doing well again, after a bad time.

works out in the end: Achieve a good final outcome.

Vocabulary Challenge

1. I'm _____ and might not graduate on time.

2. Are you going to college after _____?

3. After I _____, I can apply to the police force.

4. I can't _____ if my life depended on it! I get so nervous.

5. Tim just turned 12 and is going to _____ next year.

6. I find that it usually _____. Just be patient.

7. Can you please _____ for this meeting?

8. I think that you can _____ if you work hard for the rest of the year.

9. What are your plans for after you _____?

10. Tony and Jen get _____, but Jim struggles in most of his classes.

Answers

1. failing a class

2. high school

3. get a degree

4. pass a test

5. middle school

6. works out in the end

7. take notes

8. get back on track

9. graduate from college

10. good grades

Experts

A professor is talking to her TA about organizing a panel of experts to discuss an issue.

Professor: I'd like to **convene** a **panel** of **experts** to talk about the **decline** of the Church in Canada over the last few **decades**. I'd like for you to work on finding people to take part in it. Maybe a **dozen** or so. I'm thinking of March 3rd, next year.

TA: That sounds like an interesting topic. Were you thinking of people from the **public sector** or the **private sector**?

Professor: Either is fine. I have a few contacts in mind. I'll give you an introduction, so you're not contacting them **out of the blue**.

TA: Okay. And what **format** were you thinking about? In-person or virtual?

Professor: I prefer in-person, but we'll have to see what the university says about that in light of Covid-19.

TA: Okay, I'll keep it flexible then when I contact people.

Vocabulary

convene: Get people together for a meeting or conference.

panel: A group of people, usually experts who answer questions or discuss a certain topic.

experts: People with lots of knowledge about a specific thing.

decline: Reduction.

decades: Periods of 10 years.

dozen: 12.

public sector: Refers to people employed by the government.

private sector: Refers to people who work in private businesses.

out of the blue: Unexpectedly.

format: The way something is done; organizational structure of something.

Vocabulary Challenge

1. Why don't we _____ the vice-presidents tomorrow at noon to discuss this?

2. What's causing the _____ in bird populations here?

3. There will be about a _____ people in each lab section.

4. People that work in the _____ usually have excellent pension plans.

5. Guess who called me _____? My old boyfriend.

6. Are you going to that _____ on new treatment methods for Covid-19?

7. Public universities have been underfunded in Canada for _____ now.

8. I'm leaning towards working in the _____ after I graduate.

9. What's the _____? Multiple choice, fill-in-the-blanks, or true/false questions?

10. If you only want _____ to advise you on this project, make sure they have the qualifications, experience, and talent.

Answers

1. convene
2. decline
3. dozen
4. public sector
5. out of the blue
6. panel
7. decades
8. private sector
9. format
10. experts

Tariffs

A professor is talking about an essay assignment in an Economics class.

I'm going to spend the next few minutes talking about your final essay assignment. You have to take a look at **subsidies** or **tariffs** for an agricultural product in any country you choose and explain the **impact** it has on that industry. Choose wisely as not all countries and products have **sufficient** information to get a complete picture. Your **objective** is not to present a **unique perspective** on it but to present **complicated** economic information in an easy-to-understand manner.

It should go without saying that I expect you to cite your references carefully using the correct style. I'll penalize you **harshly** for not doing this. Please bear in mind my **grading criteria** which you can find on the class website. Your TA will be able to answer any questions you might have during your **tutorial** in the next couple of weeks.

Vocabulary

subsidies: Money given by the government to producers of a certain product.

tariffs: A tax paid to import or export a product.

impact: Effect.

sufficient: Enough.

objective: Goal.

unique perspective: An interesting or unusual way of thinking about something.

complicated: Not easy to understand.

harshly: Strongly, but in a negative way.

grading criteria: Rules and/or conditions for how something is assigned a grade (A, B, C, etc. or a %).

tutorial: Typically, a one hour class where instruction is given by a TA or professor to a small group of students. It's more interactive than a lecture.

Vocabulary Challenge

1. Why is our government giving _____ to dairy producers and not organic vegetable farmers?
2. The topic is interesting, but I'm not sure there is _____ information to write a whole report about it.
3. Where can I find the _____ for this project? I want an A+!
4. Ahhh! These _____ are way too complicated.
5. The USA and Canada often fight over _____ on lumber (harvested wood).
6. You should talk to Ken about this. He has a _____ on it.
7. She grades so _____. I'm never taking a class from her again!
8. I'm not clear on the _____ of our assignment. Can you please explain it again?
9. Please remember to sign up for a _____ after class. You will meet for an hour each week after class.
10. What _____ is Covid-19 having on mental health?

Answers

1. subsidies
2. sufficient
3. grading criteria
4. instructions
5. tariffs
6. unique perspective
7. harshly
8. objective
9. tutorial
10. impact

Confusing Words: Imply/Infer

imply: A verb that means to suggest or say something in an indirect way. Hinting at something but not directly saying it.

I didn't mean to imply that you were bad at writing.

He basically implied that I was terrible at my job.

In her latest press conference, the top doctor in Canada implied that Covid-19 wouldn't go away for years.

You can imply whatever you want, but I know the truth about the matter.

infer: A verb that means to come to a conclusion based on indirect evidence or an indirect suggestion. It's making an educated or informed guess about something.

It's easy to infer that A is better than B based on the evidence.

My wife is a genius at inferring peoples' feelings based on their facial expressions.

My husband came home with a big shopping bag. It led me to infer that he'd bought my birthday present that day.

You can easily infer what might happen next in the story, I think.

Vocabulary Challenge

1. You can _____ that vegetables are healthier than any other food based on the evidence.

2. I _____ that my husband wasn't a good cook, and we had a huge fight about it.

3. Take a look at the results. What can you _____?

4. Are you really wearing that tonight? (Jane is _____ that she doesn't like the outfit choice).

5. Look at what they're wearing. It's easy to _____ that they're wealthy.

6. The lion escaped from the cage. What do you _____ might happen next in the story.

Answers

1. infer

2. implied

3. infer

4. implying

5. infer

6. infer

123

Cover Up

Lindsay and Keith are talking about a political scandal.

Lindsay: Did you hear about that **cover up**? The prime minister got caught red-handed, finally.

Keith: I did. It was all over the news. At least he didn't **get away with** it this time. He also had to **hand over** all his tax records for the past 10 years.

Lindsay: The worst thing is that he kept **pointing to** his ex-wife, blaming her for all of this. I can't believe he **sustained** that scam for so many years.

Keith: He **screwed up**, big-time. I won't **put it past** me, that's for sure. I'm never voting for him again.

Lindsay: It's time to **stand for** something!

Vocabulary

cover up: Hide something.

get away with: Not get in trouble for bad behaviour.

hand over: Give something to someone.

pointing to: Blaming.

sustained: Kept going.

screwed up: Did something wrong.

put it past: Forget.

stand for: Have principles.

Vocabulary Challenge

1. I think there's a _____ here somewhere. It's all so suspicious.

2. Please _____ the keys at 2:00 on Sunday.

3. Let's _____ us and try to move on.

4. Does he honestly _____ nothing? I don't trust him one bit.

5. My whole team is _____ each other, but in reality, it was Ted's fault that we lost the game.

6. The economy _____ the same growth rate this year as last.

7. She shouldn't be able to _____ stuff like that. What's her boss doing?

8. I have many faults, but I can always admit when I _____.

Answers

1. cover up

2. hand over

3. put it past

4. stand for

5. pointing to

6. sustained

7. get away with

8. screwed up

Climate Change

Tommy and Sam are talking about climate change.

Tommy: Why does Professor Kim keep talking about **climate change** in his class? It's always **doom and gloom**. The **empirical evidence** to support it isn't that strong.

Sam: Oh, I totally disagree with you. The Earth is getting warmer, and it's likely **irreversible** at this point. There's so much **evidence**. We can't **sustain** our current habits.

Tommy: Oh, we can just **innovate** our way out of it, don't you think?

Sam: **On the face of it,** science may help us a little bit, but my **prediction** is that life as we know it will be over in 100 years or less if we don't **shift gears** in a radical way. Anyone can **infer** that it's just going to get worse in the future.

Vocabulary

climate change: The Earth getting warmer as a result of humans.

doom and gloom: A negative way of looking at things.

empirical evidence: Usually scientific knowledge gained by observation or experimentation.

irreversible: Can't be changed back.

evidence: Facts that prove something is true.

sustain: Support.

innovate: Make something new.

on the face of it: Without knowing all the facts or the complete picture.

prediction: A guess about the future.

shift gears: Change speed/direction or course or action.

infer: A guess or prediction based on evidence and reason.

Vocabulary Challenge

1. I think that _____ is the biggest issue facing our world today.

2. The Earth can only _____ our current habits for another decade or two.

3. We need to _____ to save the Earth.

4. Climate change is probably _____ at this point.

5. You need to support your argument with some _____.

6. You can't _____ fast enough to reverse this issue.

7. The _____ supporting that climate change is so strong. Who could deny it?

8. What's your _____ for the final exam? A? B? C?

9. _____, it looks like it was Ted's fault.

10. I don't know for sure, but I can _____ that it's going to be a future problem.

11. Sorry to be all _____ about the environment. But, there's really no good news.

Answers

1. climate change

2. sustain

3. shift gears

4. irreversible

5. empirical evidence

6. innovate

7. evidence

8. prediction

9. on the face of it

10. infer

11. doom and gloom

The Start-Up

John (internship student) is talking to Kerry (his boss) about his internship.

Kerry: How do you think your first three months here have gone?

John: It's been interesting working at a small **start-up**. You guys were **in full swing** by the time I **got on board**. But, the team helped me get up to speed and then it was **smooth sailing** from there. I've learned so much—way more than I ever learned in classes at college.

Kerry: That's great. You did well after the initial training period. Right now, we're talking to an **angel investor** and are looking to **ramp things up**. The **game plan** is to bring more people on, and we'd love to have you on the team. When do you graduate? Of course, we'd **compensate you accordingly**.

John: I graduate in August. That sounds like a **win-win** situation for both of us. You can **count on me**. I'd love to have a job lined up before I graduate and **work my way up** with this company.

Vocabulary

start-up: A company that is small and new or very young.

in full swing: Moving quickly; operating at full capacity.

got on board: Joined the team or company.

smooth sailing: Everything is going well.

angel investor: A wealthy person who provides money to a start-up.

ramp things up: To increase speed or capacity.

game plan: The plan for the future.

compensate you accordingly: Pay someone well.

win-win: Everyone involved benefits in some way.

count on me: Depend on me.

work my way up: To start at the bottom and work hard to move higher up in a company.

Vocabulary Challenge

1. I'm starting at the bottom, but I think I can _____.

2. It's tough to join a new team when it's already _____.

3. We had some logistical problems at the start. but it's _____ now.

4. Don't worry boss! You can _____ to do a good job.

5. Let's _____ for hiring with the holiday season approaching.

6. My goal is to always present a _____ situation to my clients.

7. I've never worked at a _____ before.

8. We're actively looking for an _____ so that we can open new stores.

9. Once Tom _____, I felt way more confident that we could meet our goals.

10. I'm going to take that job if they will _____.

11. What's the _____ for our presentation? Should we schedule a meeting to discuss it?

Answers

1. work my way up

2. in full swing

3. smooth sailing

4. count on me

5. ramp things up

6. win-win

7. start-up

8. angel investor

9. got on board

10. compensate me accordingly

11. game plan

Give Out

Craig is talking to Tina about his essay grading.

Tina: Hey, how's your grading going?

Craig: Terrible. I hate grading essays. My university requires that I **mark down** every single little mistake and prove why I gave every grade that I did. It **takes up** so much time.

Tina: Why not **give out** an A to everyone?

Craig: I have to **grade on a curve**. I wish I could do that! I'd be the most popular professor. Honestly though. I dread **handing back** the papers.

Tina: Could you **put up** the grades online and not **deal with** it?

Craig: Unfortunately, no. The point is that the students can see their mistakes and **learn from** them. It's not ideal, but it's what I have to do. I hope that we **transition** to computer grading sooner, rather than later. But that may **distort** grades if not implemented properly.

Vocabulary

mark down: Write.

takes up: Uses; requires.

give out: Distribute something.

grade on a curve: Assign marks according to a certain percentage of A/B/C, etc.

handing back: Returning something.

put up: Post.

deal with: Handle.

learn from: Gain knowledge from something.

transition: Change from something to another thing.

distort: Misrepresent.

Vocabulary Challenge

1. Please _____ the changes that you make. I want to know what you did.

2. I don't want to _____ this right now. Can we talk about it later?

3. My new puppy _____ all my free time these days.

4. How is the _____ to that new computer system working out?

5. Will you help me _____ my pictures this weekend?

6. I find it quite difficult to _____.

7. I'm worried that my realtor might _____ the true condition of my house, and I could get into trouble.

8. It's okay to make mistakes, but the key is to _____ them.

9. Let's _____ full-size chocolate bars for Halloween this year! We'll be so popular.

10. Teachers must hate _____ tests. There are always disappointed students.

Answers

1. mark down

2. deal with

3. takes up

4. transition

5. put up

6. grade on a curve

7. distort

8. learn from

9. give out

10. handing back

131

It's not rocket science

Meaning: Something that shouldn't be that difficult to do.

Origin: Came into common usage in 1980 as rocket science is considered to be something difficult to master. Before this, the common phrase was, "It's not brain surgery."

Example TOEFL question: Do you find your work challenging?

Possible answer: *It's not rocket science*, that's for sure! But, there are small ways in which I can increase efficiency, so I challenge myself to do that.

It's time to face the music

Meaning: Deal with the reality of something bad that you did. For example, getting punished for a crime.

Origin: From the USA in the early 1800s. Various theories:

- Related to stage fright.
- Related to the drumbeat that was played when a soldier was removed from the military for bad behaviour.
- Related to a soldier going into battle to face the music of the opponent's guns.

Example TOEFL question: Is corruption a big problem in your country?

Possible answer: There's lots of corruption in _____. *It's time* for some of the big companies *to face the music* and pay their fair share of taxes.

It takes two to tango

Meaning: There are two people responsible for a situation or problem.

Origin: First came into common usage with the 1952 song by Al Hoffman and Dick

Manning, "*Takes Two to Tango.*"

Example TOEFL question: Do labour unions play an important role in your country?

Possible answer: Not really, and I don't think they're needed. *It takes two to tango*, right? Employees can just find another job if they don't like the salary or conditions at their current job. The minimum labour standards set out by the government are quite robust.

Keep this under wraps

Meaning: Not tell anyone; conceal something.

Origin: From horse racing in the late 1800s. Refers to slowing down a horse by wrapping the reins around the hand in the beginning and middle of a race to hide the true speed. Then, they will have the strength for a sudden burst of energy at the end as they cross the finish line.

Example TOEFL question: Do you think stronger privacy laws in your country are necessary?

Possible answer: Not at all. In Canada, I sometimes think privacy laws are too strong. Some things shouldn't be *kept under wraps* in the interest of public safety for example.

Keep your head above water

Meaning: Trying to just break even. Having a hard time with something difficult.

Origin: Unknown but is likely related to struggling to keep your head above water so that you don't drown.

Example TOEFL question: Are you usually quite busy at work?

Possible answer: It depends on the time of year. Around the holidays, we struggle to *keep our heads above water* but then it slows down in January.

Confusing Words: Sight/Site/Cite

These words are homophones.

sight: A verb that means the act of seeing. Or, a noun that means vision or the ability to see.

My dog is losing his sight. The vet said that he might be blind within a year or two.

Did you catch sight of any penguins when you were there?

The sailor caught sight of land and hollered down to his friends, "Land ho!!!"

site: A noun that refers to a place. Often used with other words (website, campsite, etc.). Less commonly used as a verb that means to fix something in a particular place.

Which campsite did you end up choosing? I decided on #3.

My company is looking for a new site for their head office.

The guest house is going to be sited behind the main house (used as a verb).

cite: Most often used as a verb, meaning to make reference to something. Often used in academic settings (cite your references). Citation is the noun form and means an official government or institutional document.

Please cite your references using APA style.

The mayor gave a special citation to awoman who saved a child from drowning.

The prosecutor cited numerous experts as evidence.

Vocabulary Challenge

1. My _____ is going. I need to get some glasses.

2. He _____ an out-of-date research paper.

3. Which _____ did your company end up choosing?

4. The _____ from his commanding officer mentioned his extreme heroism.

5. You have to _____ your references carefully in college papers.

6. We're so lost! Tell me if you _____ any major landmarks or trail signs that tell us how to get back to our campsite.

7. Let's book _____ #17. There's space for a few tents.

Answers

1. sight/eyesight

2. cited

3. site

4. citation

5. cite

6. sight

7. campsite

Talking About Strategy

Mason and Owen are talking about Optic Computing, a company they've chosen in a stock market competition for an economics class.

Mason: I'm hoping that Optics Computing can gain some **market share** over ABC in the next few months.

Owen: ABC? They're **small fries** in my opinion. I'd love for Optics to gain the upper hand on XYX. I think it's **within their reach** if they can **ramp-up** production quickly enough on their new phone.

Mason: To gain on XYZ is a **long shot** for sure. But, it's potentially a **gold mine** if they become **top of mind** in the lower-end smartphone category.

Owen: Well, let's hope that Optics can **give them a run for their money**. But, we can't forget about QRS from China. They're trying to move into that space as well and have a great **team** of **product developers**.

Vocabulary

market share: A percentage of the overall market that a company holds.

small fries: Not important in relation to bigger things.

within their reach: Something that is possible. Can be obtained without too much difficulty.

ramp-up: To increase quickly.

long shot: Something that's unlikely to happen.

gold mine: Lucrative.

top of mind: The first thing people think of; the greatest priority or concern.

give them a run for their money: Try to win in a competitive situation and take first place.

team: Group of people who are trying to accomplish a goal.

product developers: People who come up with ideas for new products.

Vocabulary Challenge

1. I know it's a _____, but I'm hoping to make a million dollars in sales this year.

2. Let's _____. They're struggling right now, and the timing is perfect for us.

3. Google is _____ when it comes to search.

4. Coca-Cola and Pepsi are constantly fighting for more _____.

5. Let's _____ production on the black shoes. They're selling well.

6. You're going to join Tom's _____, starting next month.

7. I think the targets are _____ if they push hard next quarter.

8. Developing software for businesses is potentially a _____.

9. What's going on with our _____? They haven't come up with anything new in months.

10. Those guys? I'm not worried. They're just _____.

Answers

1. long shot

2. give them a run for their money

3. top of mind

4. market share

5. ramp-up

6. team

7. within their reach

8. gold mine

9. product developers

10. small fries

Cheating

Anne and Bobby are talking about one of their classmates who got caught cheating.

Anne: Did you hear about Tim? They might **suspend** or **expel** him.

Bobby: No, I'm so **out of the loop**. What happened?

Anne: I don't know the whole story, but **the gist of it** is that he got caught **plagiarizing** a paper. It's in the hands of the **administration** and the Business department chair now.

Bobby: That's pretty **harsh**, isn't it?

Anne: Maybe. But, there would be **widespread** cheating if they didn't **impose** some **standards** for this kind of thing.

Bobby: I guess you're right. **The other side of the coin** is that probably everybody cheats a little bit though. The Internet makes it so easy.

Vocabulary

suspend: A temporary prohibition against attending school.

expel: Permanently prohibited from attending a school (sometimes limited to a specific number of years).

out of the loop: Not knowing the latest information or gossip.

the gist of it: The summary or highlights.

plagiarizing: Copying something.

administration: People in charge of something (university, government, etc.)

harsh: Very strong.

widespread: Something that's everywhere or something that everyone is doing.

impose: Force something to be put into place.

standards: Level of quality; expectations.

the other side of the coin: A different way of looking at a situation.

Vocabulary Challenge

1. Are they going to _____ Kara for cheating on the test?

2. My professor is quite _____ when it comes to grading papers.

3. Well, _____ is that he failed a class, so he won't graduate this year.

4. Tony loves to _____ his crazy ideas on his students.

5. Are there any rumours going around? You know how _____ I am.

6. My students think I won't notice them _____ something in their essays, but it's easy to catch them.

7. Well, _____ is that her professor has a bad reputation as well for ignoring student emails.

8. How can I get in touch with the _____ from the Psychology department?

9. There was _____ anger about the decision to close that dormitory.

10. My professor has high _____, but I don't mind. I've learned a lot in her class.

11. Can they _____ someone for cheating on just one exam?

Answers

1. suspend

2. harsh

3. the gist of it

4. impose

5. out of the loop

6. plagiarizing

7. the other side of the coin

8. administration

9. widespread

10. standards

11. expel

By No Means

Tory is talking to her friend Kim about her business.

Kim: How's business these days?

Tory: Well, manufacturing costs in Canada are so high that we're considering moving it to China or somewhere else in Asia. We can produce products **at a fraction** of the cost. Cheap labour is **abundant** there.

Kim: What about quality? How can you control that?

Tory: Well, we're starting **on a small scale** and will know **in time** whether or not it's high enough. **By no means** do we want to produce inferior products. You have to be careful to **select** the right company to work with.

Kim: That sounds sensible.

Tory: **In the end**, we just can't turn a profit by manufacturing in Canada or the USA. We will have to **cease** our North American operations soon.

Vocabulary

at a fraction: Something way smaller or fewer.

abundant: Present in large quantities.

on a small scale: A small operation or output.

in time: After a while.

by no means: Certainly not.

select: Choose.

in the end: Eventually.

cease: Stop.

Vocabulary Challenge

1. _____ do I think you should quit. Just finish your degree!

2. You can buy that _____ of the cost online.

3. You need to _____ the right program if you want to get a good job after you graduate.

4. We need to _____ production of the ABC line. Sales are just too low.

5. I produce vegan products _____ in my home.

6. Social media experts are _____ in Vancouver. We have so many choices for who to hire.

7. You'll know _____ whether he's the one for you.

8. _____, we had to fire him.

Answers

1. by no means

2. at a fraction

3. select

4. cease

5. on a small scale

6. abundant

7. in time

8. in the end

Balance of Power

A student is giving her opinion about Canada's changing society in class.

Immigration is causing **the balance of power** to **shift** in Canada. Most people are not coming from other Western countries, but they are **refugees** coming from countries with a lot of problems. Because of this, we're undergoing a massive change in society. The groups of people who used to be **visible minorities** even just 10 years ago are now in the majority.

The big problem is that the highest levels of the government and institutions don't reflect this change. **The powers that be** need to be willing to **relinquish** some control and make a **concerted effort** to include these increasing groups of people in decision making. If they don't, it could **trigger** massive **social upheaval** within the coming decades. This is something that is happening **across the board** in Europe as well.

Vocabulary

the balance of power: All groups have roughly equal power.

shift: Change.

refugees: A person forced to leave their home country due to a natural disaster, war, etc.

visible minorities: A group who looks different from most people in a certain place.

the powers that be: The people in charge/at the top.

relinquish: Give up.

concerted effort: Serious attitude and action for a task or goal.

trigger: Cause.

social upheaval: Sudden or violent change.

across the board: Applying to all; sweeping.

Vocabulary Challenge

1. _____ is always changing in Europe, depending on who is running the EU.

2. Oh, you know how _____ are at this university. So cheap and will do anything to save a buck (a dollar).

3. There are lots of _____ from Syria in Vancouver now.

4. I don't think you've made a _____ to study for your test yet.

5. The university is making some budget cuts _____.

6. _____ can have a difficult time in small towns in Canada.

7. Let's talk about the _____ that caused this to happen.

8. I know you don't want to _____ control, but he is 18 now.

9. The US is going through a lot of _____ right now.

10. Let's _____ gears. I'd like to talk about . . .

Answers

1. the balance of power

2. the powers that be

3. refugees

4. concerted effort

5. across the board

6. visible minorities

7. trigger

8. relinquish

9. social upheaval

10. shift

Gold Standard

Jen is asking Katrina for some help with her Psychology essay.

Jen: Katrina, you're good at writing, right? Could you have a look at my essay and give me some **feedback**?

Katrina: Sure, let me have a look. Okay . . .well, you're **on the right track**. Your **task** was to explain the differences and similarities between cognitive psychology and behaviorism?

Jen: Yes, exactly.

Katrina: You've **utilized** resources well. But you could certainly **vary** your sentences to make it a bit more interesting. There's no certain **formula** or **gold standard** for good writing, but I try not to use the same words over and over. You use "very good," "for example," and "When I compared" at least 10 times each. It's kind of **repetitive**. Use some substitutes instead.

Jen: Oh, I didn't even know I did that! So to **summarize**, make my writing more interesting!

Katrina: Yes, my **rule of thumb** is to use these kinds of phrases only once or twice.

Vocabulary

feedback: Input about something.

on the right track: Heading in the right direction.

task: Job; something to do.

utilized: Used.

vary: Change; mix up.

formula: A way or method of doing something.

gold standard: The best or most reliable version of something possible.

repetitive: Happening again and again.

summarize: briefly give the main points.

rule of thumb: A broad guide or principle.

Vocabulary Challenge

1. Did your professor give you _____ yet about that project?

2. Try to _____ the phrases you use during your presentation. It can get boring to hear the same thing over and over again.

3. It's an easy _____, but it's almost too easy. I'm so bored!

4. To _____, your quality is good, but you need to speed up a little bit.

5. The _____ is no errors whatsoever. Make sure you proofread well.

6. I think I'm _____, but I won't know until I talk to my professor.

7. There must be a _____ for this. Let me have a look before we start.

8. My _____ is to start projects as early as possible.

9. My job is kind of _____, but I'm allowed to listen to podcasts.

10. I loved that project at work. It _____ a lot of my skills.

Answers

1. feedback

2. vary

3. task

4. summarize

5. gold standard

6. on the right track

7. formula

8. rule of thumb

9. repetitive

10. utilized

Factory Farms

A student is commenting on climate change in a class.

I think that all our discussion about climate change **overlooks** one important thing— what we eat. **Cattle** production on **factory farms** releases a massive amount of **methane gas** into the atmosphere, not to mention polluting the local water sources. This is important because it's something that individuals can have an impact on, and it's time to **come to grips with** this. We need to eat less meat!

The good news is that there is a shift happening in consumer awareness. More and more plant-based meats are **in the pipeline,** and they are becoming increasingly popular with consumers. These new kinds of "meat" have the potential to **transform** the way we eat. I'm **under no illusion** that we'll suddenly have more Vegans because people are worried about climate change. However, plant-based meats **have a lot of potential** if two or three times a week, people choose it instead of beef, pork, or chicken. People would be healthier too! And, meat consumption is already in **decline**.

Vocabulary

overlooks: Fails to notice something.

cattle: A name for cows (more than 1 of them).

factory farms: Large farms that operate on a huge scale.

methane gas: A kind of gas that's released by cows as they digest food.

come to grips with: Begin to deal with.

in the pipeline: something being developed by a person, company, government, etc. that will be available soon.

transform: Dramatic change.

under no illusion: False idea or belief.

have a lot of potential: Has the ability to change into something else in the future.

decline: Decay; a reduction.

Vocabulary Challenge

1. I'm _____ that this situation will get better.

2. The _____ outside my city pollute the air, land, and water.

3. We have to _____ the fact that climate change is real.

4. The numbers of international students have been in _____ since the pandemic.

5. _____ is a major contributor to climate change.

6. I want to _____ this piece of land into an organic farm.

7. He _____, but he needs to focus on his studies instead of playing video games.

8. We have a similar product _____. It should be available in about 6 months.

9. I'm so thankful that my teacher _____ so many errors in my writing.

10. I grew up on a farm that raised _____.

Answers

1. under no illusion
2. factory farms
3. come to grips with
4. decline
5. methane gas
6. transform
7. has a lot of potential
8. in the pipeline
9. overlooks
10. cattle

Erroneous Assumptions

Bob and Sammy are talking about a group project they are doing.

Bob: Before we get too far into this, I'm having some reservations. I don't want to **disrupt** our flow, but I think we need to **amend** our data collection plan. I think we've made some **erroneous** assumptions about how easy it will be to find people to survey.

Sammy: That seems a bit **arbitrary**. Why do you think we won't be able to find people?

Bob: The **criteria** are too **precise**. I don't even know if that kind of person exists, much less finding 20 of them. We need to change our **method**.

Sammy: I don't **wholly** agree with you, but you do have some **valid** points. Can I **contemplate** this overnight and let you know what I think in the morning?

Bob: Yes, of course. Thanks for considering it. Let's chat before class tomorrow at 8:30.

Vocabulary

disrupt: Interrupt by causing a disturbance.

amend: To change for the better.

erroneous: Incorrect.

arbitrary: Based on a random decision.

criteria: A principle or standard by which something is judged.

precise: Exact.

method: A way of doing something.

wholly: Completely.

valid: Just; well-founded.

contemplate: Consider thoughtfully.

148

Vocabulary Challenge

1. Can I _____ you for just a minute? I have a few questions.

2. Be _____ in how you cut this. The corners won't match if you're not.

3. We need to _____ the bylaws at the next general meeting.

4. You do have a _____ point, but I don't think I'm going to change my mind.

5. Which _____ did you use to come to that answer?

6. I need to _____ this for a bit. I'll let you know my answer next week.

7. Don't you think that promotions at this company are a bit _____?

8. You have some _____ beliefs about evolution I think.

9. I don't _____ agree, but I think we can come to a deal.

10. What are the _____ by which we're going to evaluate job candidates?

Answers

1. disrupt

2. precise

3. amend

4. valid

5. method

6. contemplate

7. arbitrary

8. erroneous

9. wholly

10. criteria

Confusing Words: Who/Which/That

These words are all used for relative clauses but are used in different situations. The rules are not strict for which and that, and they're often used interchangeably.

who: Used for people.

Tommy is the one who really turned things around for our company.

My mom is someone who loves to help other people.

Do you know anyone who is looking for a job? I need to hire someone.

which: Used for groups or things.

Used for nonessential (non-restrictive/non-defining) clauses, often with commas.

She volunteers for a great organization, which specializes in saving endangered animals.

There's an all-natural product, which was featured in the Toronto Sun that I want to try out.

I got a new TV, which can understand voice commands.

that: Used for people as well as groups or things.

Used for essential (restrictive/defining) clauses. They add vital or very important information. These often don't use commas.

I don't trust products that claim to have "all-natural" ingredients.

Lukas is on the team that won the tournament.

Do you know someone that is reliable? I need to hire a new person.

Vocabulary Challenge

1. My sister is someone _____ is very smart with her money.

2. I bought a carpet _____ had a hole in it. I didn't notice until I got home.

3. My wedding dress, _____ I bought last week, costs $3000.

4. The person _____ did my kitchen reno did a nice job.

5. The contract _____ defines the scope of work is on my desk.

6. My computer, _____ used to work fine, stopped working last week.

Answers

1. who

2. that

3. which

4. who

5. that

6. which

Extra practice: Fill in the blanks.

My mom is someone who _____.

I work for ABC company, which _____.

I don't like products that _____.

At a Standstill

Aaron is talking to a librarian on the phone about a book he was trying to find.

Aaron: Hey, this is Aaron Smith. I'm wondering if you've found that book yet.

Librarian: Well, things are **at a standstill for the time being**. I searched **at length** in all the libraries in Canada and had no luck.

Aaron: Is it available in stores?

Librarian: More bad news. It's been **out of print** for more than 20 years, which means that it's **out of stock** everywhere. Sorry to **contradict** what I initially told you, but I did some research and just found this out.

Aaron: Oh no!

Librarian: Your best chance of finding it might be to illegally download it if you can find it. I don't generally recommend it, but it might be your only hope. You may also have to **adjust** your expectations. It will be difficult to find.

Vocabulary

at a standstill: Stopped.

for the time being: At this current time.

at length: For a long time.

out of print: More copies are not being made (usually refers to a book).

out of stock: Not available in stores.

contradict: Give an opposite opinion.

adjust: Change something to make it better.

Vocabulary Challenge

1. _____, I'm happy enough with Amy. We do have some problems though.

2. Sorry, that size is _____. How about another color?

3. We talked _____ but couldn't come to an agreement.

4. Talks between the two parties are _____.

5. Why don't we _____ that bike side? You'll have a more comfortable ride.

6. Why do you always _____ everything I say during meetings? I'm so tired of it.

7. That book is _____ now. You'll have a difficult time finding it.

Answers

1. for the time being

2. out of stock

3. at length

4. at a standstill

5. adjust

6. contradict

7. out of print

Land on your feet

Meaning: To be in a good position again after a difficult time.

Origin: Unknown.

Example TOEFL question: Do you think that the government provides enough social safety nets in your country?

Possible answer: Yes, most definitely. Sweden has several programs to help the working poor and the unemployed. Anyone who wants to *land on their feet* can usually do so.

Learn the ropes

Meaning: Get trained to do something.

Origin: Two possible explanations. The first is from people who travelled around doing rope tricks for a living. These tricks were not easy to learn and master. The second is new sailors who had to learn to tie ropes on sailing ships.

Example TOEFL question: What is a difficult job?

Possible answer: I think that one of the most difficult jobs is being a doctor. It takes a long time to *learn the ropes*, and then after that, you have so much responsibility. One mistake could result in someone dying.

Let off the hook

Meaning: To not be punished, even though he/she was caught doing something wrong. For example, a politician who doesn't go to jail even though he committed a crime.

Origin: From the 1800s and refers to a fish letting themselves off a hook to not be caught.

Example TOEFL question: Do you think the punishment for criminals in your country is strong enough?

Possible answer: In general, it's fair for crimes that cause physical harm. However, politicians often get *let off the hook* way too easily for things like corruption.

Making a mountain out of a molehill

Meaning: To make something into a bigger deal than it is. For example, someone who gets a traffic ticket but doesn't pay it and then ends up going to jail because of it.

Origin: From the 1500s in Nicholas Udall's translation of "*The First Tome or Volume of the Paraphrase of Erasmus upon the New Testament.*"

Example TOEFL question: Do you think social media platforms should be subject to censorship?

Possible answer: Honestly, no. It's quite obvious what's fake news and what isn't. People that are clamouring for this are just *making a mountain out of a molehill.*

Make ends meet

Meaning: Make enough money to pay all the bills.

Origin: First seen in the 1600s but the origin is uncertain.

Example TOEFL question: Do you think that government should be doing more to protect the environment?

Possible answer: There are two sides to it. On the one hand, lots of people are struggling to *make ends meet,* and the government should be doing more to help them. But, the longer-term issue is global warming which needs to be addressed as well.

Swallow My Pride

Nathan is talking to his friend Zeke about looking for a job.

Zeke: Hey Nathan, how's the **job search** going? Anything going on?

Nathan: Not well. I've been **applying for** jobs but no bites yet. There are so many **job seekers** out there now with the high **unemployment rate**. I might have to **swallow my pride** and take an **entry-level job**. I was hoping for something better, but that's not likely now. It's **kind of late in the game**.

Zeke: You could **do an internship**?

Nathan: Nah, I need to **earn money** now. I've got bills to pay with my massive student loans.

Zeke: **Hang in there,** my friend. Any **stable** job isn't a bad thing in this economy.

Vocabulary

job search: The process of looking for a job.

applying for: Seeking employment by sending out applications/resumes/CVs.

job seekers: People who are looking for a job.

unemployment rate: The number of people without jobs measured against the total workforce (listed as a percentage).

swallow my pride: Humble myself.

entry-level job: A job that doesn't require much (or any) experience.

kind of late in the game: Too late in the process to be useful.

do an internship: Work for free to gain experience.

earn money: Make cash.

hang in there: Don't give up.

stable: Secure; not changing.

Vocabulary Challenge

1. I want to give up on my _____. I'm not even getting any interviews.

2. _____, okay? I know it's difficult, but it'll be worth it when you're done.

3. I had to _____ and apologize to my teacher last week.

4. I'm trying to think of creative ways to _____ this summer.

5. My job isn't _____. I can be laid off at any time.

6. There's a seminar for _____ tomorrow night at the employment center.

7. Sorry, it's not possible. You're _____ for internship applications, aren't you?

8. The _____ is 3.5% in Canada.

9. I think I might _____ to get some experience.

10. Most university graduates take an _____ after they graduate.

11. My goal is _____ at least three jobs a day.

Answers

1. job search

2. hang in there

3. swallow my pride

4. earn money

5. stable

6. job seekers

7. kind of late in the game

8. unemployment rate

9. do an internship

10. entry-level job

11. applying for

Before You Go

If you found this book useful, please leave a review wherever you bought it. And please don't forget to join my email list for useful tips for learning English: www.eslspeaking.org/learn-english.

You may also want to check out these other resources (also by Jackie Bolen). It's easy to find them wherever you like to buy books.

- 365 American English Idioms

- Advanced English Conversation Dialogues

- English Vocabulary Masterclass for TOEFL, TOEIC, IELTS, and CELPIP

Made in the USA
Las Vegas, NV
06 February 2025

17673235R00087